Alfonsus Antonius de Sarasa

Compendium of the art of always rejoicing

Alfonsus Antonius de Sarasa

Compendium of the art of always rejoicing

ISBN/EAN: 9783742865366

Manufactured in Europe, USA, Canada, Australia, Japa

Cover: Foto ©Andreas Hilbeck / pixelio.de

Manufactured and distributed by brebook publishing software
(www.brebook.com)

Alfonsus Antonius de Sarasa

Compendium of the art of always rejoicing

COMPENDIUM

OF THE

ART OF ALWAYS REJOICING.

BY

F. ALPHONSUS DE SARASA, S.J.

TRANSLATED BY A LADY.

WITH A PREFACE BY THE REV. T. MEYRICK, S.J.

———————

LONDON:

BURNS, OATES, AND COMPANY,

17, 18 Portman Street and 63 Paternoster Row.

1872.

LONDON :
ROBSON AND SONS, PRINTERS, PANCRAS ROAD, N.W.

PREFACE.

THE following treatise is a compendium of the admirable work of F. Alphonsus de Sarasa, of the Society of Jesus. It was so much esteemed in Germany that the great Leibnitz, according to the testimony of Koeler, considered it to be a perfect model of composition and sound morality. Weigel, who translated it from the Latin into German, styles it 'an incomparable and golden book.'

Alphonsus de Sarasa was born of Spanish parentage in Flanders, A.D. 1618. He entered the Society of Jesus at the early age of fifteen. After his noviceship and usual course of studies, he taught humanities for seven years, was a ripe scholar, profound philosopher, and great preacher, listened to with marked attention at Brussels, Ghent, and Anvers. But his chief title to renown is his work on the *Art of always Rejoicing.*

The effort of composing so noble a production, requiring such a compass of thought and imagination, together with his labours in teaching and preaching, and his fervent piety, consumed his feeble frame, and he died of a pleurisy and decline at the age of forty-eight.

The greater work in fifteen treatises, and the compendium drawn up by himself and published with it, were printed by Meursius, at Anvers, in 1664. A new edition by Fischer, professor of the University of Jena, appeared in 1741, and was printed by Weigand at Leipsic, with notes by Fischer and Erard Weigel. The book is now very rare indeed, and deserves reproduction in any form.

The compendium made by F. Sarasa was translated in 1842 into Italian by the accomplished F. Antonio Bresciani, S.J., author of the *Jew of Verona*. From the Italian, as it is not easy to procure the Latin copy, this brief treatise has been well and faithfully rendered by a lady.

May the consolation which it is calculated to give reach thousands of hearts, and give them the sweet peace which it proclaims!

THOMAS MEYRICK.

Feast of the Epiphany, A.D. 1872.

ART OF ALWAYS REJOICING.

THE object of this, my little treatise, is to explain to you the art by which you may attain to the full possession of the joy that the Apostle commends so highly. In order to conduct you to this happy lot, it is not my intention to display fully before your eyes the whole magnificent series of the inscrutable designs and the unfathomable abyss of Divine Providence on which every human event depends, but I shall only endeavour to impress upon your mind the most sublime idea of the infinite wisdom and the supreme goodness with which God rules the world in order to persuade you to conform your will to His. This is the source of all joy. From this fountain springs that peace which overflows our heart and which keeps it quiet, tranquil, and at rest, amidst the storms

B

and turmoil of human events. I shall, indeed, have done much if, after having found where to commence in the midst of such a labyrinth of intricate matter, I am able to find the clue and to explain to you briefly and distinctly the *Art of Rejoicing*, and to put it before you in such a manner that you may see it plainly and clearly as in a glass. And what is more, having cleared away all confusion, I shall show you that this art rests upon one sole powerful argument, which is the basis of the whole stupendous fabric.

I. *That peace is to be sought within us, and not without us.*

And now, my reader, permit me to depart somewhat from the ordinary custom, and to reason with myself instead of with you. Let me occupy myself for a short time with my own affairs, and consider attentively my own thoughts.

There is a small secret apartment in my house where I am in the habit of collecting together my thoughts, and of holding converse with them. I hear outside everything in confusion and disturbance; the tumult, the tramp, and noisy cries of the people put me in fear, and I dread lest when I go out of doors I may be involved in the general disturbance of the world, and be dragged into the vortex of its torrent. I therefore take refuge in myself alone, and seating myself at my fireside I quietly call up my thoughts, which for a while have been still and dormant, like bees sleeping in their hive, and having arranged them in good order, I address them thus: ' As there is no peace, my friends, to be found amid the tumult and incessant agitation of human affairs, let us see if it can be found at home and in converse with you; for you know that true enjoyment is found only in tranquillity and internal peace, as Seneca says: "Gaudium cuique domi suæ nasci"—"Every man's joy begins at home."' In this way, kind reader, I shall draw out for you gradually the workings of my thoughts, while you will follow me; and if I succeed in finding peace in the midst of so many earthly troubles and disorders, you will have the clue which will enable you to extricate yourself from the labyrinth of human vicissitudes, and to gain that most profound peace of the soul which all wish for, and to which so few attain. And then you will, indeed, be happy!

CHAPTER I.

That the world is full of trouble and vexation.

THERE is no one who does not complain
that the world is full of annoyance and deceit.
And I can the more easily believe this to be
true, when I see that those who assert it are
so numerous, so wise, and so well versed in
affairs.   But if I ask them the cause of all this
vexation and misery, they reply with one voice,
that the bitter source of all sorrow is that
the whole world ' positus est in maligno,' ' lies
in wickedness,' and therefore everything goes
wrong and at cross purposes, since ' every man
is for himself,' ' omnes quæ sua sunt quærunt'
(Phil. ii.); and while each one seeks his own,
he gets that which belongs to others; and not
only so, but by means of theft and force, and
by trampling justice under foot, takes possession of it.   Friends are rare, and not to be
trusted, and often full of envy, calumny, and
deceit; they are friends in name, but enemies in
deed.   Thus enemies and friends are merely
interested, not real, and men put on a smile

without while the heart is false within. Nothing is done for justice, but all goes by might instead of right. The drift and purpose of every action is ambition and the desire of rule. Poverty is held in contempt, simplicity and virtue are derided. In order to attain to any higher position, it is sufficient for the schemer to be a clever flatterer, a liar, a perjurer, ready with his tongue for any invention or any deception, bold of hand, and a contemner of God and man. And when we turn our attention to our own body and soul, what constant changes do we find in their condition! Sometimes our bodies are afflicted with maladies, and O, with what grievous ones! and though we may occasionally be strong and robust, yet we are liable at any time to be attacked by sickness, and to suffer from feebleness and pain. The soul, too, has its peculiar diseases, which are severe, grievous, and full of anguish. Ennui, melancholy, anger, cupidity, aversion, hopes and fears, agitate it continually. If we look around us at those in the midst of whom we live, we see them sometimes loving us to excess, at other times hating us intensely; perhaps they help us with one hand, and humiliate us with the other; now they may crown us with praises and exalt us to the skies, and then again load us with injuries and cast us down to the lowest depths. Fortune itself is uncertain; it is seldom successful, often adverse, and always changeable. The sky does not even always look the same. At one time we suffer from the cold of winter, at another from the heat of summer; and though the heavens now may be unclouded and serene, we suddenly see them grow dark, clouds cover them, the wind whistles, the lightning flashes, the thunder rolls, hailstones rattle on the ground. Hence arise dearth, destruction of the corn, pestilence, dreadful diseases, and sudden deaths. And how can I describe domestic and public discords? In the courts of law I see a crowd of litigants, hustling one another, and pressing round the bench of the judges, while the conclave echoes with a thousand outcries, like the noise and roaring of the sea during a storm. Again, the violence of war destroys and lays waste provinces and kingdoms; so that everything in the world is in a state of unceasing agitation. How, then, can peace be found amid such tumult, such groans and tears, such misery and ruin? How can I find any rest at all in the midst of such a universal commotion?

II. *That there is only one thing in the world which afflicts us, and this is the opinion that nothing is done as it ought to be.*

This is what is said continually up and down in the world, and quite seriously and with a grave countenance. When, however, I turn my eyes within, and reason seriously, I resolve henceforth not to listen to what people say. For I see that the world makes an unjust accusation, and that the ten thousand evils which the multitude see in the world can be reduced to one. And this is to be found in myself alone, and through my own fault. It is a certain idea which has taken possession of my mind, and is the origin and the exciting cause of all my disquieting thoughts. Epictetus warns me to beware of it when he says, ' Homines turbantur non rebus, sed iis quas de rebus habent opiniones'—' Men are troubled not by things, but by the opinions they have about things.' And the mischief of such ideas consists in this—that I wish to see everything done according to my fancy; and because this does not happen, I am annoyed at everything, nothing pleases me, and I am filled with anger and indignation. Just reflect for a short time, and see if this be not the case. You ask me why I feel annoyed; and I reply, because nothing is done well, but everything goes wrong. Well, and suppose everything were done as you wish it, and as you have pictured it to yourself? O, in that case it would be different; then things would go on smoothly. Thus you see I do not vex myself because the world goes wrong, but because it does not go according to my idea; so that if I had only the power of turning it round as I wished, then, though the earth fell from its poles, though the rivers ran backwards, though the sea were dried up, and the mountains removed, though the earth quaked, and everything were turned topsy-turvy, I should look on calm and unmoved in the midst of it all, and should amuse myself with smiling at the ruin. And why should I feel thus? only because all this took place by my will. Then those things would please me which now I censure and disapprove of, since what pleases one does not disturb one's peace. I can now therefore no longer say, as I did before: The world goes wrong, it is a swarm of vexations, a cess-pool of misfortunes; it is a valley of tears; I shall say instead : Nothing in the world is done rightly and properly, because nothing is done as I would have it : this is the sole well-spring of all my troubles.

III. *That in order to have peace, we must correct this folly.*

If, then, I could henceforth get rid of this idea (whether good or bad we need not in-quire), if I could banish it from my house and home, and, conforming my own mind to the universal opinion of mankind, I could approve of whatever is done, and of the way in which it is done, and if I could accustom myself to wish things thus and not otherwise, I cannot see that anything would for the future disturb my peace of mind, not even if the heavens and the earth were to be turned upside down. But what if they were? Why, still I would say all is well. But it ought not to be so. What concern is that of mine? Let those who are vexed at it dispute about it. We shall see afterwards who is wrong. Meanwhile, whether it be well or ill, I think as I do; and this is enough for my peace of mind. Find fault still, my friends, but nothing will change my belief that what happens as I wish will make me most happy; and I wish that it may happen as it does; for it is my opinion that it ought to happen thus, and not otherwise.

IV. *Suppose that everything happens as you would have it, and you will have peace.*

It has been, then, up to this time a strange delusion of mine, that, in order to attain to peace, I wished everything out of myself quiet, and I did not know how to restrain and calm the tumult of my fancy within me. If I calmed this, everything would be calm. It would indeed be absurd in any person who desired to reach some place by sea, if he were to wish that the winds should not blow, that the sea should become calm, that the shrouds should not creak, that the sails should not be set, that the oars should not ply, that the sailor-boys should not ascend the rigging, that the sailors should sit still, that the pilot should not direct the helm, but that all should compose themselves in the profoundest calm, and quietly go to sleep: certainly such a person would wish that which could not be attained; and if it could, it would be to his disadvantage; for without movement no progress could be made, and the ship would remain stuck fast, as on a sand-bank. If he wish to sleep in the midst of the raging of the sea, the roaring of the wind, the hauling up of the ropes, the groaning and the creaking of the ship, the going to and fro of the sailors, the chattering, the scolding, and the clamouring of the passengers, he must curb his imagination and go down quietly below deck, leaving all to make their own noise at their posts; he must distract his mind, impose silence on himself, and wrap himself up in his cloak, and then he will enjoy the sweetest repose in the world. The case is exactly similar. Let things take their own course. And why, indeed, need I foolishly trouble myself about everything, and mix myself up in every concern? Why puzzle my brain, and become so confused in my thoughts, letting them wander without rule, and judge of everything, and censure the actions of other people? Do I, indeed, wish to adjust and to arrange all that takes place in the world? What folly! for while I am endeavouring to set others right, I only vex and irritate myself.   What, then, shall I do in order to feel at peace?   Simply what Epictetus advises: ' Non postulabo posthac ea quæ fiunt arbitratu meo fieri, sed ut sapiam, ita fieri quæque volam, ut fiunt'—' I will no more ask for everything to be done according to my will, but for wisdom to will that all should be done as it is done.'

To change the will of others is not in my power, to bend my own is.   If hitherto nothing has been done as I wish it, I will henceforth wish that all may be done as it is done.   And this wish will be most easy, if I correct this one opinion, and believe that everything which happens in the world is right.   If I attain to this, although the world turn upside down, my soul will always possess unchangeable peace.

CHAPTER II.

That the world is apparently in disorder.

BELIEVE me, the case is as I have stated it. Be it so; what you say sounds well, but here is the difficulty: and who will explain it?   How can I think that all proceeds rightly, and in order, when I see everything go to ruin? You din into my ears the praises of nature, calling it most wise. This is nonsense. Most wise indeed! It is still more changeable and variable than ever. Consider, as I said before, how inconstant is the sky of heaven. To-day there is not a breath of air, and you have a suffocating heat which enervates the body. Next day there are blasts and whirlwinds, which root up and carry along with them the trees of the forest. Now mountains are struck by lightning, now there are furious storms at sea, and hail breaks the branches of the oaks and beats out the standing corn. At one time of the year the frosts are very sharp and prolonged; at another the heat of the dog-days parches the ground and dries up the springs; it withers the fruit, kills the herds, and impregnates the air with pestilential vapours: and must I think that all this takes place by rule, by law, by wise arrangement, and not rather by chance, by caprice, and by accident? If I next turn to consider human events, how can I think that all there works rightly? Is not everything full of falsehood, of perfidy, and of feigned friendship? And are not the courts of justice filled with litigants, and are not kingdoms contending with each other in war? Are not the worst of men the most prosperous? To them is chiefly opened the road to court, to dignities, and to riches, which is closed to the good; the former holding a high position, the latter having to be content with a low place; the one enjoying pleasures to the full, the other pining in poverty and want. And is not everything governed blindly by chance? And has any one ever heard chance call itself wise?

I. *That it is not necessary to know the reasons of things in order to judge of them.*

In the voice of another I gave utterance to my own thoughts. Seeing that the world, notwithstanding its confusion and disorder, has yet lasted for so many centuries, and that it is not flung from its poles by the disturbance and disorder of human events which will continue as long as the world lasts, I begin to suspect that some great mind governs the universe and rules its movements, though in an invisible manner. Then it occurs to me to think of what would happen to a person who, ignorant of the art of navigation, should find himself in a vessel at sea. If, while the ship sailed across the wide expanse of ocean, the said passenger were sitting under cover, and watching with surprise the work of the sailors, he would see some ascend the mainmast, others seat themselves on the spars, others climbing from rope to rope as far as the maintop; some furling one sail, some unfurling another; here giving quarter to the wind, there setting the staysail; now lowering the mainsail, or spreading out the foresail full to the wind; others meantime tightening or loosening the cords, laying hold of and drawing in pulleys, engaged at the wheel, pumping out the hold, or taking the soundings with the lead. Then all in a moment the vessel's bows are turned to the right or to the left, as the wind blows; and suddenly, while the ship is in balance, she is thrown on one side, and almost resting on the waves, and in an instant gliding along, she cuts through the water, which bathes her sides so that they appear to be immersed. The poor passenger is frightened at seeing so many different operations and strange and sudden movements, and he calls out to this or that sailor, and tries to stop him and inquire why all this is done. The sailor is occupied and does not listen to him, nor, if he replied, would the passenger, who is ignorant of the art, understand him; and each instant the poor man, fearing and trembling, thinks he will fall headlong into the sea. But on entering the poop-cabin, he finds the old pilot, concentrated in thought, with the helm in one hand, the compasses in the other, and his eyes fixed on the chart of navigation. Now he sees him measure with the quadrant the elevation of the sun, and follow with exactness the degrees on the meridian; now consider on the mariner's compass the polar deviation, then count out the knots in order to learn the speed at which the vessel is going, then compare on the scale the distances which the map indicates; and when he sees here and there astrolabes, chronometers, telescopes, and sextants hanging from the walls, and looks in astonishment at the ephemeroids and the tables of declination, refraction, and elevation, and when he observes that the pilot makes use of all these things to guide the ship, and not only so, but that he also gives orders from his small chamber, and that the crowd of sailors obey him silently and respectfully, then at length all his fear leaves him, and he believes that everything is ordered rightly, and with great wisdom. But does he therefore understand the reason of the orders given? Certainly not. And why does he now feel safe, though he was so afraid before? Only because he now believes blindly and entirely in the skill and wisdom of the pilot.

II. *That it is sufficient to know that all is governed by God.*

Is it not as I said? One such thought alone is able to calm a man even in the jaws and at the hour of death. Why, then, should I vex myself by searching into the reason of everything? And why grow angry at seeing the world in confusion? And why torment myself by examining into so many things, and by endeavouring to set them right? I will act otherwise. I will flee far from the noise and the tumult of human events, and raising my thoughts above, I will consider things in a more exalted sphere, searching if there be not some mind which watches over and orders all that takes place in the world. The eternal portals

c

roll back, and with eye dazzled at first I enter
with David into the sanctuary of God, where
the deep and inaccessible counsels of His paternal providence are discussed in the presence
of Infinite Wisdom; and there within, though
hidden in an abyss of light, I see, with St.
Augustine, 'nihil fieri sensibiliter et visibili-
ter, quod de interiori illa aula non jubeatur
aut non permittatur'—'that nothing is done
in the world of sense and sight which is not
by command or permission from that invisible
court.'   Behold, in that majestic temple there
appears to me 'antiquus dierum Deus, et vide-
bam in conspectu suo habere omnes vias meas'
—'the Ancient of days, and in His sight are all
my ways, and those of all men.' The prophet also
exclaims with astonishment at the sight, 'Thou
knowest my sitting down and my rising up,
and Thou hast known all my ways.'   'Behold,
Lord, Thou knowest the first and the last; and
in Thy book all are written.   Lo, Thou hast
numbered my days.'   'Thou, Thou, my Lord
and my God, searchest into everything, and
with Thine omnipotent sight penetratest the
most hidden recesses; and Thou dost work all
things in number, weight, and measure.'   I am

filled with astonishment, and while worshipping Thee prostrate on the ground, I admire, O my God, the sublimity of Thy mind which governs me. Fool that I was, to believe that anything happened by accident, and that chance presided over events and ruled the world!

III. *That a man will have peace if he form the highest conception of God.*

If I have the highest opinion of this most wise Mind, which governs, orders, and rules everything, I can easily bear each human event with calmness; it is a divine Mind, and that is sufficient for me, because I have the highest opinion of its wisdom. Epictetus, although a heathen, speaks of it thus: 'Religionis erga deos immortales, præcipuum illud est, rectas de eis habere opiniones; ut sentias et eos esse, et bene justeque administrare omnia'— 'It is a chief part of religion towards the deities to have right opinions about them; to believe that they exist, and that they govern all things justly and well.' From which it follows, 'parendum esse eis, et omnibus iis quæ fiunt acquiescendum et sequendum ultro, ut quæ a mente præstantissima agantur' (Epict. *Ench.*

38)—' we must obey them, and acquiesce in all things which are done by them, taking them for the best, as being done by a mind of consummate wisdom.' There is no necessity to understand all the causes of human events in order to judge if they happen rightly; but while sweetly trusting in God, I must confide all things to His loving and wise providence. The passenger who set sail ignorant of the art of navigation, did not suddenly know how to guide the ship because he saw the instruments and the calculations of the pilot, nor did he guess the use and the nature of those instruments, of which he knew not even the name; but from the sight of them there arose in his mind admiration, admiration led him to have the highest opinion of the pilot, and this high opinion calmed his mind, which was agitated before by a thousand fears.

IV. *By considering the instruments which God makes use of to rule the world, you will acquire a high conception of God's power.*

In order to impress upon my mind the highest opinion of the great wisdom of God, it is not necessary to contemplate God Himself in His essence—and who could do so?—but only to consider the means which He makes use of to organise and direct the machinery of the universe. Nor, in order to do this, need we think of the finest, the most recondite, and the most elaborate of the instruments, but of those which are the most manifest, the most ordinary, and the most simple. I look up and consider the vast expanse of the sky, which, like a rich pavilion ornamented with stars, covers and adorns the immense sweep of the firmament. And then I see the sun enter as the king of light, with all the splendour of its countenance, shedding its rays, its heat, and its light all around; its rapid revolutions moving concentric and eccentric on the ecliptic. I behold the order of its rising and setting, of its advancing and receding between the tropics and the equator, in order to form the different seasons of the year, the measurement of time, the distinction between day and night, and the computation of years and centuries. The earth presents other phenomena to the eye of the observer, and I see everywhere mountains and plains, indentures of its shores made by the action of the sea, and slopes from the summits

of the highest mountains, in order to give a
course to rivers, and reservoirs in caves and
caverns to afford a constant supply to springs.
Here the earth is clothed with ancient forests,
and there it spreads out into cultivated lands,
and germinates everywhere, affording a thousand kinds of food to domestic and to wild
animals. I notice amongst so many closely-
allied variations of nature, that the greatest
does not destroy the least, nor the highest
injure the lowest, nor does proximity mingle
those nearest together, but all work together
in harmony. I am astonished at the sight of
so many wonders, and exclaim: ' Cœli enarrant
gloriam Dei, et opera manuum ejus annuntiat
firmamentum ;' ' magnus Dominus, et lauda-
bilis nimis, et sanctus in operibus suis '—' The
heavens declare the glory of God, and the
firmament showeth the work of His hands ;'
' great is the Lord, and to be praised exceedingly, and holy in all His works.' And while
I am full of admiration and praise of the infinite wisdom of God, who rules the world,
would you not think it absurd if some foolish
person were to whisper in my ear, ' O, my
brother, I should be wrong not to blame you

for praising God for that which He has not done : chance is the great architect of the world, and collects the atoms wandering through space, unites them, and enables them to form themselves into all that which you so much admire in nature.' Should we not tell such a foolish person that the atoms must have formed his brain badly? He had better go and relate such nonsense to old women in their dotage, but not to any one who has a grain of sense in his head. Let him tell *them* that the beautiful harmony and order displayed throughout creation is not the work of a divine Architect, but that chance rules the world, and orders all things. Has such a one looked on the shores of the ocean, and seen the grains of sand carried to the shore by the billows during a storm? Has he ever seen them, amid all this boiling and foaming of the waves, form themselves into a beautiful palace — the minute particles forming large stones for the foundation, others building the walls, and here and there leaving openings for windows; others taking the form of bases, and others the round shafts of columns; others curving themselves into arches, or making pedestal, capital, or architrave? Has he seen them take the fantastic forms of light carving or decoration, and form the faces of lions and bulls' heads?

Has such a dreamer ever seen chance geometrise, and form such a palace as I have described above? He would never see the sands form so much as a fisher's cabin; and does he wish to make us believe that the beautiful proportion, symmetry, and wonderful harmony of the world's fabric, is not the work of a sovereign Mind, but accomplished by chance?

How, too, shall I speak of the movements of the heavenly bodies, and describe the power which urges them forward incessantly, and attracts them to the centre, making them rotate rapidly both with a simple and compound movement, and always in harmony with each other, with advancings, recedings, and influxes which in time and measure form but one music and a celestial dance?

If, moreover, I observe that the most glorious bodies are not created to delight in their own beauty, but in order to be instruments in the hands of God, to preside over nature, and to render it fruitful,—O, then, full of the highest admiration, I exclaim, 'Magnificata sunt opera

tua, Domine, et nimis profundæ sunt cogita-
tiones tuæ'—'Great are Thy works, O Lord,
and Thy thoughts are exceeding deep.'

Is it not clear that light emanates from the
sun, to revive, to adorn, to colour, and in various
ways to rejoice the world? The sun is the
cause of the alternation of day and night. By
its oblique position, either in Cancer, or high
up in Capricorn, or lower down, the zones are
either torrid, or temperate, or frigid. The sun
causes seeds to grow, roots to spring up, stems
to sprout afresh; by it leaves are coloured,
fruits ripened, flowers tinted, ice melted. By
it animals warm to love, nightingales salute it
from their nests, lions and tigers from their
caves, frisking colts from the meadows, butter-
flies from the flowers, insects from the herbs,
fish from the depths of the sea. The sun is
the cause of clouds, tempests, whirlwinds, rain-
bows, lightning, winds, snow, and rain. It
lights up the inaccessible peaks of mountains,
and hardens and colours gems and marbles.
It is the cause of all the brilliancy of diamonds,
the green of emeralds, the golden colour of
amber and topaz; it causes the sky-colour of
the beryl, the blue of the lapis lazuli, the ver-

milion of the ruby, the whiteness of the pearl, the pale colour of the sapphire, the azure of the turquoise, the blood-colour of the jasper, the eyed face of the onyx, the wavy look of the agate, the spotted surface of the porphyry, the speckled, striped, and veined appearance of the many various kinds of marble. The moon too works incessantly for the benefit of nature. She tempers the heat of the sun, regulates the months, presides over agriculture, fertilises seeds, invigorates plants, changes the winds, dissipates or condenses the clouds, and also in a mysterious manner causes the flow and ebb of the tides. Such instruments in the hands of God, and directed with such order for the good government of the world, commend to us highly His sovereign wisdom, and make us repose tranquilly on the loving breast of so provident a Father, who by His benefits consults our greater good, and that continually by ways sometimes patent to our eyes; but more often hidden; for, as is said in Ecclesiasticus, 'Multa abscondita sunt majora iis; pauca enim videmus operum ejus. Benedicite, ergo, omnia opera Domini, Domino; laudate et superexaltate eum in sæcula'—'Many things are hidden greater than these; for we see few of His works. Then, O all ye works of the Lord, bless the Lord, praise and exalt Him for ever.'

CHAPTER III.

That everything in the world is directed by Divine Providence.

WHILE I am thus filled with admiration and pious feelings, the doctrine of the old physical philosopher provokes my disgust which denies that there is any providence of God in the world below, but makes it only extend as far as the moon, and then confine its sphere of operation to the space between it and the firmament, giving motion, light, and harmony to the stars. He assures us that it would not be worthy of God to cast His eyes so low, and to cloud them with the dust of this earth, nor would it be fitting that He, who is so majestic and grand, should take the trouble of making the grass grow, of giving flowers their beautiful colours, of curling the endive, or of infusing odour into the thyme, the goat's-rue, and the cinnamon. Worse

still to make Him nursing-father to young lions,
colts, and chickens, to make Him hatch the ova
of the fly, the gnat, the flea, and watch over
vile insects, in order to disperse abroad the
putrid matter of dead carcasses. 'What,' he
asks, 'has God to do with such infinite minutiæ? Would He not be equally great without having to uphold the earth under the shock
of an earthquake, or to still the raging of the
sea, or calm the winds, or send rain upon the
earth? Suppose it were to enter your mind to
make Him come down at any time to number
the drops of the ocean, or the atoms of the air,
or the grains of sand, in order to get Him to
place them in a spot here or there! Truly 'tis
a mean idea of God! Leave Him rather in
heaven, to measure the immense sphere of the
stars and their orbits; to arrange their circuits,
to adjust their centre of gravity, to moderate
their impetuosity, and to trace out their road.
Yes, leave Him in heaven. It is clear also that
He takes no care of mankind; for when we
see them act so imprudently, and grope, as it
were, in darkness, we know that God has left
them to themselves. For if He watched over
them, we should not see such difference of for-

tune, nor such terrible misfortunes; neither would so much daring wickedness not only go unpunished, but oftentimes appear to be rewarded.' Thus say the impious in the words of the Stagyrite, whose brain in this case has a taste of the moon's influence. But tell me, you who make the moon a barrier to Divine Providence, and thence with your dull argument pretend to drive Him from the earth below. You say that God's highest perfection consists in walking about through the heavens, and in regulating and giving movement to those highest and most noble orbs, without ever deigning to turn His eye to this earth, to see if things are going on rightly, or to stretch forth His omnipotent hand to govern them well. You who are so clever in syllogisms, let me see if you can solve the following question. Listen. Would any artificer display all his care in making his instruments exact, beautiful, and ornamental, and then not take care of the work which he models by the means of these instruments? Or have you ever seen the beautiful statues sculptured by Policletus, and when he had finished them, and given them their last touches, did he leave them without care, amongst the dust and the spiders, and go to caress the chisels and the files? And did Apelles, who painted your Alexander so excellently, frame the pencils and gild the paint-pots, and hang them up to adorn the walls, leaving meanwhile his exquisite canvas to be gnawed by mice? What do you answer, friend Aristotle? You laugh, and I laugh at you, and at your blunders. Let us suppose again that a skilful watchmaker put together a watch, with much study of its various parts, such as the wheels, the pivots, the springs, the pendulum; that he placed all the pieces in their right position, and set the exquisite piece of machinery in motion; and that after all this trouble, he cared not whether the hand pointed to one hour or to another, but looked upon such minutiæ as unworthy of his noble intellect. Would it not be foolish in any one to act thus? And if such conduct would be ridiculous in the watchmaker, it would indeed be unworthy of God, the all-wise Creator of the world.

I. *That God takes care of the smallest things.*

If I turn my eye again towards the earth, and consider what is taking place in its sphere,

I see clearly that no cloud rises in the sky, or breath of wind blows, no meteor is bright, or drop of dew descends, without the instrumentality of the sun; without its action not a blade of grass grows, not a leaf buds forth, not a flower blossoms, no fruit ripens. The sun causes the silvery appearance of the moon; this latter presides over night, and is able by its influence to produce a thousand effects on water, plants, and animals. I see that without the sun eternal darkness would cover the earth, and extinguish in it all life and heat; it would become either a mass of mud or of thick ice. And who will persuade me that God governs only the heavenly bodies, and cares not for earthly things, when we know that He has created and set the sun in its position, in order to give them form, to enliven, to nourish, to increase, and to preserve them; and when we see also that He has neither placed the sun so high as to chill the earth, nor so low as to set it on fire; that He has not placed it in this or that fixed spot, so that one hemisphere would have perpetual day, and the other perpetual night. He gives the sun its oblique path in the ecliptic circle in order to cause the different seasons of the year; and while in one part of the earth fruit-trees are only budding into blossom, in another their fruits are ripening; and in the adjoining parts the corn is fit for reaping, and the fruit for gathering; while in the still colder portions of the earth, where the sun's rays penetrate less and more feebly, nature seems almost asleep. The stars themselves, which hang at infinite distances, hardly give a tremulous ray of light to the earth; as if tracking the path of the sun, they accompany him in his wanderings, and give names to and divide the months and the seasons. The constellation of Aries opens the new year; that of Leo rises with the sun in the heat of summer; that of Libra, mitigating the sun's heat, renders the month of September mild; that of Capricorn lengthens the nights, and gives rise to hoar-frosts and intense cold.

And does, then, God solely take pleasure in the instruments which He makes use of in such a wonderful way for the good of the earth, and will He not watch over the earth itself with the greatest care? You repeat that it is unworthy of God to regulate such small matters. I will not reply. God Himself shall answer you; God, so jealous of His glory, shall speak to you from out the whirlwind which envelops Him, and say: 'Quis est iste involvens sententias sermonibus imperitis? Accinge sicut vir lumbos tuos: interrogabo te, et responde mihi. Ubi eras quando ponebam fundamenta terræ? Quis posuit mensuras ejus, si nosti?'—'Who is this that wrappeth up sentences in unskilful words? Gird up thy loins like a man; I will ask thee, and answer thou Me. Where wast thou when I laid the foundations of the earth? Who laid the measures thereof, if thou knowest? Who shut up the sea with doors? Tell me, if thou canst. Was it not I who put it within confines and barriers when I said: 'Usque huc venies, et non procedes amplius'?—'Hitherto thou shalt come, and shalt go no further.' Didst thou ever bid the day to dawn, or shake the extremities of the earth? Have the gates of the abyss of the kingdom of death been opened to thee, or knowest thou where the light dwelleth, or hast thou entered into the storehouses of the snow or hail? 'Indica mihi, si nosti'—'Tell me, if thou knowest.' Everything obeyeth My bidding, and I alone rule over all; not only over that which thou esteemest

D

great, but also over that which appeareth little in thy poor sight. 'Quis est pluviæ pater, vel quis genuit stillas roris? Quis præparat corvo escam suam, quando pulli ejus clamant ad Deum?'—'Who is the father of the rain, or who begot the drops of dew? Who provideth food for the raven when her young ones cry to God?' Fool that thou art! 'Numquid contendis cum Deo?'—'Dost thou contend with God?' (Job xxxviii.) And to speak the truth, why should you think it unworthy of God to watch over an animal, while you consider it glorious that He rules the sun? 'Pusillum et magnum ipse fecit, et æqualiter est illi cura de omnibus' (Sap. vi.)—'He hath made both great and small, and hath a care alike of all.'

Nay, rather, if we consider the matter well, He perhaps displays greater power in forming a gnat than in creating the sun, which being without life, gives light to others, and does not itself possess the power of sight. Does not the structure of a gnat strike you as marvellous? Look at this small creature; see it balance itself on its wings of gauze, and move them rapidly so as to cause a humming in the air, and then give forth suddenly a shrill trumpet-like sound.

I observe that its wings are clothed with a transparent tissue, and with network, and small muscular fibres, which enable them to bear up against the motion of the air; the head, placed above the body, is very light, and at its extremity there is a small and indescribably fine proboscis, at the top of which you can see a little mouth, provided with a lancet and suckers to pierce through the skin and extract the blood which it feeds upon. It is enough to make one wonder to watch the quick movement with which it draws this out of its sheath and extends it, and the cleverness with which it extracts the blood, and draws the sucker up with the act of swallowing, and having got the mouthful, swallows it, and makes it pass into its body, and there digests it, and forwards it through imperceptible passages for nourishment.

It is all formed of such a fine and delicate fibrous texture as to feel the least impressions of the air. Observe how lively this little insect is; how it is attracted by the smell of food; watch it resting on its long and nodous legs, and swaying to and fro, and showing off its beauty; and does not God appear as great to you in giving light, defence, and nourishment to this little insect, as in clothing the sun with light? And does it not appear less wonderful that He gives movement to the sun than that He puts together the small machinery of this tiny frame?

Run through in your mind the vast number of other insects even more minute than this, and you will find all wonderfully organised, and all having wherewith to feed, defend, clothe, and adorn themselves. Look through the finest microscope, and you will see on every blade of grass, however smooth it may look, in every drop of water, on each petal of a flower, an infinite number of small insects which are imperceptible to the naked eye. But why do I tell you to make use of a common microscope, simple or compound? This is not enough. I will bring before your sight numberless other tribes of insects. Have you ever had an opportunity of seeing the immense magnifying power of a solar microscope, which possesses the power of making a flea look as large as an elephant? Well, place under that lens a minute particle of cheese, the size of a millet-seed. See it so increased in size as to appear a transparent rock. Look more closely, see how it swarms with life. Who would have thought it? How many inhabitants people that small space! They are insects, and though magnified so highly, they do not exceed the size of a lentil-seed. This piece of cheese contains an entire world: valleys, mountains, caverns, pastures, hiding-places from the plots of the more powerful; some live in a solitary state; others in families and make laws for themselves; others lead a wandering life, and live as they like. I see some feeding, some setting out in quest of amusement, some creeping into caves, some gambolling, some drinking; there is one, who has the worst of it in a combat, and I notice how it twists itself about, bites, and chafes; the conqueror stands over it, tears it with teeth and claws; some run away; others fly to give help, and so the fight is rekindled. O omnipotence of God! Whenever I see this wonderful spectacle, I feel my heart full of a thousand affections. And you who so foolishly deny the providence of God, are you not convinced, and will you not adore the wisdom of God in small matters as well as in great? I ask you in the words of St. Augustine, 'Quis disposuit, quis

fecit ista?   Expavescis in minimis: lauda magnum.   Qui fecit in cœlo angelum, ipse fecit in
terra vermiculum'—'Who hath arranged, who
hath done all this?   Thou art full of fear at
these least things.   Praise Him in His greatness.
He who made the angel in heaven maketh the
worm upon earth.'

CHAPTER IV.

In order to excite in us this high opinion of God's power,
we must contemplate His threefold knowledge.

I MIGHT possibly think that God, who has
to attend at the same time to such a number of
different things, and so far removed from each
other, might perchance err through forgetful-
ness, inadvertency, or ignorance.   First, therefore, humbly asking leave of His divine majesty,
I enter farther into that august and mysterious
conclave of the sanctuary of God, and there
contemplate the threefold divine knowledge.
O Lord, my God, how many and what won-
drous things do I see therein! and yet not only
am I unable to follow and to read all, but I

scarcely can scan rapidly the titles of the books.

Science of Intelligence.

The first science which meets the eye on entering this stupendous sanctuary is that which theologians call the ' science of simple intelligence ;' and they give it this name because it works nothing external to itself, and stops in pure perception. What an abyss! This science comprehends every possible creature; all possible infinite worlds, including our own; all the endless species of creatures, and the endless number of individuals of each species; infinite angels, infinite men, infinite animals, who will have no being but in the mind of God alone. And thus I see that this science, in fact, so much belongs to God, that without it He would not be God. Because, if He knew no other possible creatures beside those which He creates; these being created, He would not be able to create other fresh creatures, because He would know no others; for no one can form anything without having first conceived the idea of it in his mind. I see, also, that all such cognitions are not diverse in God, and some succeeding others; but all simultaneous, clear, distinct, and unchangeable. Thus I see clearly, that all such indivisible acts are nothing else but God Himself; so that if one only were taken away, God would no longer exist.   Whence it also appears that this science is absolutely necessary to God, in order that He may be able freely to create what He pleases.   And I said freely; for if He wished to create the world, as He did create it freely, would He have been able to do so if He knew no other possible world except this? He could not do that of which He was ignorant.   And where there is no choice, there is no freedom.

Science of Vision.

Going still deeper into my contemplations, I discern the ' science of vision,' as theologians call it, by which all things which were to take their rise in the mind of God, and to have existence, were seen in an instant by God clearly from all eternity, as if already called into being, and present to Him.   Hence the history of every creature, present, past, and to come, is described by His omniscient eyes; all the story and circumstance not only of men but of animals, of herbs, of stones, of atoms, so that even the life of a tiny ant is delineated and divided into chapters and paragraphs. From what tribe it is descended, who its parents were, where it saw the light, and the place, the day, and the hour of its birth are all noted down. Also what it did day by day, what it ate, where it dwelt, what battles it had with its enemies, and the place and the manner of its death. Nothing escapes that eye, which even occupies itself with the exact history of a little ant. And in like manner the histories of all creatures are written and divided into lines, chapters, and volumes, for God sees them all distinctly as it were in a looking-glass. For if He failed even in the knowledge of a grain of sand, He would no longer be God.

Science of Conditional things.

And what shall I say, lastly, of that divine light, which, according to theologians, comprehends the ' science of conditional things'? It is so deep, and extends so far, as to be almost infinite in each and every single created thing. Thus God does not only know what I am now doing, or shall do hereafter; but He also foresees what my thoughts would be, and what I should do in that place, or at that time, in prosperity or adversity; He knows what I should do at Rome or at St. Petersburg, at Meaco or at Mexico; in the courts of kings or in the dwelling of the poor; in the populous metropolis or in the deserts of the Hottentots or the Laplanders. And as the circumstances which might happen to me are infinite, and the combinations of persons and things which could take place with regard to me alone are infinite, so it is clear that the conditional knowledge which God has of me alone is also infinite, while the knowledge which He has of all possible contingencies is, if I may use the expression, infinitely infinite; and, as I said before, this knowledge is in God, clear, distinct, and evident, and all simultaneously comprehended in the twinkling of an eye. Will not, then, what has been said, and according to the poor capacity of our thoughts and language darkly shadowed, more than suffice to awaken in our minds the most noble, the most august, the most immense idea of the consummate wisdom of God? If thou art wise, adore simply, because thou understandest it not.

Let it be enough to have scanned for a moment the profound abyss of knowledge whereby the mind of God governs with such deep counsel us and our affairs. Yes, for this little insignificant man alone, for this handful of dust, this little piece of clay, God puts in exercise such mighty arguments, such profound thoughts, such infinite wisdom. And this atom, this piece of dirt, dares to be proud in the sight of the Omnipotent, and fixing its weak gaze on the inscrutable abyss of the divine intelligence, would fain fathom at a glance the sea of His knowledge, and the designs of His providence!

Ah, Sovereign Creator, my Lord and my Keeper, I am confounded, and throw myself lovingly into Thy arms; 'for all Thy commands are justice; in wisdom Thou hast done all things' (Ps. cxviii. 103).

CHAPTER V.

That everything happens by the supreme design of God.

THE thought that God regulates all human events with infinite wisdom, is of great use in composing the mind to peace. It would be of little avail to the pilot to be well acquainted with the art of navigation, if he could not practically make use of it to guide the ship to the port; and sometimes even although he can do this, the ship does not obey him readily, either from the fury of the winds, the raging of the sea, the unshipping of the helm, or from some other unforeseen cause. But it is not thus with God. He knows how much effectual action is necessary in order to direct the universe, and He can do what He wishes, because no obstacle can oppose itself to the Almighty. I see that before creating a world, He thought of all possible worlds in order to select that which He wished of His own free will to draw out of nothing. In the same way, wishing to create me, He cast His eyes on all possible men, ran through the history of each, and compared them with me in every possible way. He

weighed all circumstances, and selected me for
creation at His own time, and as if reading the
catalogue of those who were to be created, He
called me by name with a loud voice. This
. was the signal for my creation: ' He said, and
they were made' (Ps. cxlviii.). Just as my
voice in the articulation of the word ' sun,' by
expressing the idea of that heavenly body,
brings it before the mind of him who hears
me pronounce it, so in the same way I only
exist by the express word of God. While I
read it merely with my eye, the word ' sun' is
in my mind alone; if I say the word, this idea,
which before was but a conception of my intellect, is formed in the mind of him who hears
me. In the same way, before God has spoken,
He sees in His mind the possible creature;
when He speaks, He has already created it.
Besides, just as the word which I pronounce
depends upon my voice, so that at one time
it sounds longer or louder or more subdued,
as I may wish by my way of pronouncing it,
so all creatures whatsoever depend on the voice
of God; for if God were to cease existing or
speaking, they would all perish in an instant,
just as my words would cease if I were silent:

' By the word of the Lord the heavens were framed, and all their power by the breath of His mouth' (Ps. xxiii.).

I. *That nothing which takes place in nature happens by chance.*

Thus my mind has acquired more clearly the knowledge that nothing in nature happens by chance; but that, on the contrary, everything proceeds, is regulated and governed by the highest skill, the greatest wisdom, and the fullest knowledge. For if chance is nothing but an unforeseen event, and far from what would have been expected, how can a casual accident have place in God, if He, by His infinite wisdom, foresees all possible events? For if we turn to consider merely natural operations, and those which have no dependence on the free will of man, it would be absurd to think that they are the offspring of chance, when we see that God created so many celestial bodies to regulate events. Therefore we should not say that winter, summer, rain, wind, drought, proceed from mere chance, when we know that God in His great wisdom disposes secondary causes in such a manner as to produce them alternately. It is only an aberration of the brain to confuse chance with wisdom. And do not actions, which proceed from the free will of man, happen by God's disposing providence? We read in Scripture, that having often foreseen them, He described them to the prophets many years before, and they came to pass afterwards exactly as He had predicted. How could He know of them so long before, and with such certainty, if chance, and not His divine mind, had directed them?

The providence of God, in order not to interfere in the least with man's free will, having foreseen in the immense volume of events, and well weighed, how each person would have acted under such or such circumstances, selected those circumstances and that position in which man could use his free choice in such a way that his free action should lead infallibly to that which God, in His wisdom, had foreordained. For if you look at the proximate cause leading to the result, it may often appear to you to be chance; but if you wish to enter into the mind of God, who remotely disposes the said causes, you will understand clearly the deep counsel which produces that effect. I see it in the history of Joseph, as in that of many others. He interprets dreams, he accuses his brethren; his father loves him, he is ill-used by them. They entrap him, throw him into a well, and cruelly sell him. At first he is made much of in Egypt, then cast into a dungeon like a felon, and then into the stocks; and we see him at length, instead of suffering misery, enjoying greatness as a saviour of the kingdom and of his father's house. God wished such a termination; and it was attained through means apparently unfavourable. Read here your own history, and you will find there in all the finger of God.

II. *That we ought to consider all well done which is done by God.*

This being the case, as it really is, why should I feel disturbed about human events, when I see infinite wisdom presiding over and ruling them? Am I so foolish as to believe that God does not know what is best to be done; or that though knowing it, He does not wish to do it; or that wishing it, is not able to do it? How can I be so inflated with pride as to think myself more farseeing than God

Himself? Do I wish to make myself His coun-
sellor and director; to show Him His mistakes
and to teach Him to act with greater wisdom;
I who cannot draw a single drop of rain from
the clouds? I should have a much more exalted idea of divine wisdom if I did not venture
to blame that which it commands, or even to
doubt the wisdom of its counsel. From henceforth I will be silent and adore. Let there be
thunder or lightning, rain or drought; let the
winds roar, the winters be severe, the summers
hot; let the earth be fruitful or without a blade
of grass; let the animals pine away; let the air
be full of infection; let wars rage; I will certainly approve of everything. Nor can I do
better than spare myself the least doubt as to
that which depends on God's will being the
best. He rules over everything from all eternity, and He knows how to turn causes and
effects, so as to make His greater glory shine
forth, for the increase of which all things work
together in admirable harmony; 'for the Lord
has made all things for Himself' (Prov. xvi.).
And if He does everything for and by Himself,
cease to say that He can act otherwise than
rightly.

E

CHAPTER VI.

That God turns to good the evils of the universe.

HAVING considered the way in which divine wisdom rules the world, I now turn to notice the complaints which blind mortals make against God's providence; and I see that these, far from diminishing God's glory, only serve to increase it. These objectors ask if it is worthy of God to bear with the extreme wickedness of sinners? Homicides, adulteries, poisonings, cheatings, treacheries, blasphemies, perjuries, and, the worst of all crimes, idolatries; these wound God's honour most deeply; and surely if He occupied Himself with mankind, He would not permit such dishonour to His sovereign majesty. Thus do those short-sighted people speak who cannot penetrate the counsel of God.

But I see clearly that although men run riot in a thousand pleasures, God wisely permits this in order to preserve inviolate their liberty of action. He created them free, and considered it worthy of His wisdom to let them know that He would not on any account infringe upon their sacred right of liberty. For it is great glory to a noble emperor in receiving unforced homage from poor and abject slaves; but surely greater glory to receive homage from free vassals, who are themselves barons, and who, of their own free will, do him homage. God had no lack of obedient servants; all the inanimate creation, and that part of the animate which is deprived of reason, praises and submits itself to God its Creator; but it does this by the law of necessity. Demons, even though fretting in chains and in torments, bend down before Him and proclaim Him king. Angels, absorbed in contemplation of the divine beauty, prostrate themselves before Him with willing but not with free homage. God wishes both for voluntary and for free subjection, and therefore He selected man to give Him more exalted glory. As in His sovereign wisdom He gave man liberty, so in order to preserve this liberty intact, it was also necessary to permit wicked actions, if He wished for free homage.

Also His glory shines forth more clearly through these same wicked actions; for if there had not been sin, God the Son would not have clothed Himself in human flesh, nor would He have offered Himself to divine justice on the altar of the cross. For from that death more glory accrued to His offended Father than all the actions of sinners had deprived Him of. His glory was increased, because, were it not for the perverse wickedness of the sinner who breaks His commandments, God's dominion and jurisdiction would not be manifest to us; nor His generous patience in bearing with the sinner, nor His mercy, which inclines Him to pardon, nor His infinite love, which receives him when penitent, and having welcomed him back, admits him to the former place in His love and regard, whence these high and clear attributes of God are displayed before mankind. I see plainly therefore that God's glory is augmented by the wickedness of sinners, instead of diminished, as you think. And not only is this the case, but you are to observe that God orders the evil actions of the perverse for the good and for the use of men. The patience of the elect would not shine forth so vividly without the smoke and darkness caused by the malice of the reprobate, which like a shadow throw it into relief. But for the cruelty of tyrants, there would not be such a long line of martyrs to give glory to God; nor would the Church be rich with so many invincible champions, if God had not permitted her to be tried long and severely by the wickedness of evil-doers. Hence the battles of patience and the victories of courage both conduct us to an eternal crown; whilst, on the other hand, even the wicked themselves, who are tormented unceasingly in hell, will, with gnashing of teeth, glorify the justice of God. Whence, I observe, that human wickedness turns to the highest glory of His divine majesty; for, as St. Augustine excellently remarks: 'For Almighty God—as the heathen allow Him to be—the Lord of all things, being supremely good, would by no means permit any evil to be in His works unless He were so omnipotent and good, that He would bring good even out of evil' (*Ench.* x.). 'Non enim Deus omnipotens (quod etiam infideles testantur, "rerum cui summa potestas"), cum summe bonus, nullo modo sineret mali aliquid esse in operibus suis, nisi usque adeo esset omnipotens et bonus, ut bene faceret etiam de malo.'

CHAPTER VII.

That we ought not to feel indignant at the prosperity of the wicked. God permits it in great wisdom.

I NEXT turn to consider the other complaints which fill the mind and agitate it extremely, and I hear men scornfully ask, 'Why is the path of the wicked prosperous, and why is God silent while the wicked devoureth the man that is more just than he?' (Hab. i.) Why do the wicked rejoice, while the good are sad? Why does fortune smile on the former, and deal hardly with the latter? Instead of joining in these complaints, I view the matter in a different light; for the joy of the wicked, far from extinguishing my faith, only makes it burn the brighter; for it teaches me that after this life a new life awaits us, in which God will reward virtue with everlasting happiness, and punish sin with everlasting pains. He, being just, will not punish everything in this life, just as He will not reward everything in it.

Besides, in accounting for such inequality of fortune, it will be a great comfort to your mind to consider that the fool often esteems those

things to be blessings or misfortunes, which in
reality are not blessings or misfortunes. 'For
this,' as Seneca says, 'is the design of God, to
show to the wise man that the things which
most men desire and fear are neither good nor
bad; they will seem to be good if He give
them only to the good, and bad if He give them
only to the bad. (*De inv.* v.) So, then, the
good things which are given only to the good
must needs be of another kind;' and this also
awakens the sweet hope of a future life.

And why, then, do I continue fretting and
disturbing my mind so much about the unequal
division of pleasures and of good fortune? For
if I consider the matter, I see clearly that there
is no reason why the wicked should be excluded
from good fortune, or why good men should
be the only fortunate ones; for if the wicked
were to be fortunate to the exclusion of all
others, they would give themselves up to sin,
drawn to it merely by pleasure; whilst, on the
contrary, if the bad were excluded from all
enjoyment, grown wicked out of despair, they
would become doubly rebellious against God,
through rage at His chastisements; besides, being irritated and exasperated through misery,

evil-doers, thieves, and homicides, might overwhelm human society, and destroy both human
things and divine.   Nor would it be wise that
the good alone should enjoy every good; for,
inebriated with delights, they might easily turn
aside from the path of virtue, and fall by degrees into sin ; as, on the other hand, it would
not be fitting that all the good should be miserable, for then divine worship could not be
protected by the rich, or guarded in a fitting
manner from its irreverent and bold opponents.
Therefore I ought in no wise to complain of
the inequality of fortune, which I see is ordered
rightly by divine wisdom, so as to maintain inviolate the order of the universe.

CHAPTER VIII.

*That there must be a great variety of dispositions and
of humours.*

No less was my folly in being disturbed
by seeing so many different dispositions and
inclinations amongst mankind; as if it were a
misfortune to meet continually with inexperi-

enced, giddy, mad, and foolish people. Here I
see a person of a melancholy,. unhappy, cross,
and sluggish temperament; there is another
who is possessed of a lively, sanguine, and
volatile one; some persons are easily moved
to anger and passion; others are cold as ice
and chilling; some are foolish, some hasty,
some jovial, some fond of joking, some talkative, some silent. Is it not an extreme annoyance and weariness to be obliged to live amongst
those who possess such different natures and
dispositions?

Would it, however, be the happiest state
of existence to pass one's life in conversing
with men of the same genius, temperament,
and disposition as one's own? What an extravagant idea! The other day I was tan-
gibly made sensible of my folly, while saunter-
ing through the city, and the thought came
into my mind to separate the various classes
of citizens, and to disperse them in different
quarters, each according to his nature: here
the choleric, there the morose; on this side the
foolish, on that the learned; here the talkative,
there the combative; and then elsewhere the
wise. I found that I had never erred so much

as when I thought myself so wise; for I saw
that such was the fickleness of human brains,
that they would not continue stationary for an
instant, and therefore it was impossible to
arrange them in different classes.   Besides,
without this variety of professions and of dispositions, social intercourse would soon cease,
or at least life would become a misery and
weariness.   For if all were equally rich and
of an equally subtle intellect, who would there
be to serve and to be in subjection to their
betters?   Who would apply himself to me-
chanical arts, or to cultivating land, or to building, or to merchandise?   Who would prepare
our food, or weave cloth, or provide the other
necessaries of life?   And yet without these,
men would live like the wild animals of the
forest, deprived of the refinements and the ad-
vantages of social life.   Thus God makes use
of such diversities of fortune for the benefit of
man, so that some amongst mankind are obliged
to exert themselves in the service of others in
order that they may get their living and pro-
sper.   In the same way He forms the different
dispositions of mankind, in order that each, as
his talent leads him, may give himself up to

whatever art suits him the best; this it is which gives rise to such a variety of pursuits, of machinery, of ornaments, of business, of trades, of amusements, of sciences; all these make the world so pleasant, varied, and magnificent. If we add to these the variety of the powers of the body, and observe that some persons are weakly, some delicate, some stout, and some so strong as to bear any fatigue, we shall find that all are suited for different exercises, and that this variety of dispositions and of strength, of riches and of poverty, of governing and of subjection, is proportioned and given us by God, with so much forethought and counsel, that we should not be set against it, but, on the contrary, be fully content and entirely approve of it.

CHAPTER IX.

That we ought also to approve of public calamities.

HAVING laid down these general observations as the basis of our reasoning, I turn my eye and thoughts to the particular events which may take place in human affairs. And, first

of all, I consider the calamities which happen
to a country, such as seditions, wars, the sub-
version and the ruin of provinces, and that
which most of all distresses and wrings my
heart, the seeing that so many evils happen
through the folly of princes, or the cowardice
of soldiers, or the arrogance and bad advice of
those in high place. But if I look more closely
into the merits of the case, I see that such disorders are decreed by God, who disposes rightly
not only of men, but of the most extensive kingdoms. The course of human events is such,
that happiness without alloy does not last long;
for even the states which were of such ancient
origin and such high destinies were overturned
at last and demolished. God transfers the good
fortunes of one country to another, and makes
them vary continually, like the waves of the
ocean, lest by a long state of prosperity they
should overwhelm the world.

Why, then, am I so surprised at hearing
of wars, or at seeing enemies spread themselves, like inundations, over provinces? Fortune changes its abode, and enemies, like
porters, in the form of soldiers and plunderers,
carry it elsewhere. Does even a private citizen

ever leave his old home quietly? Must there not be the noise of wagons and conveyances to carry away his possessions? And how can the fortunes of provinces and kingdoms change quietly and without tumult?

I will therefore not trouble myself to accuse either the bad counsels of rulers, or the insolence of magnates, or the quarrels of princes, or the cowardice of soldiers, or the rebellions of subjects. All these are only instruments which God makes use of to change the prosperity of kingdoms, as a punishment for the crimes of the people. It is their wickedness which gives the enemy power; ' for by our sins the barbarians are strong,' as St. Jerome says; and on account of the wickedness of subjects God sometimes casts down the best of kings from their thrones, and banishes them from their realms. It is our evil deeds which deprive kings of counsel, ministers of wisdom, soldiers of their strength, citizens of concord. As God therefore sends us these disasters as chastisements for our good and for our greater merit, it only remains for us humbly to bow down and kiss, without a murmur, the just and paternal hand which strikes us. For St.

Augustine truly says, ' God seems to be angry
when He does these things. Fear not, He
is not angry to destroy. He is more angry
with thee when thou livest ill and He spares.
All these tribulations are the rod that scourges,
lest it be the sentence that condemns' (Ps. lxv.).

CHAPTER X.

That every one ought to be contented with his own state of life.

HAVING considered things which take place
external to myself, in public and in private, and
which are ordered in accordance with divine
wisdom, and being fully convinced of their just
and proper procedure, I enter my house finally
in order to find out whence come the many dis-
turbances which throw it into such disorder.
And I collect together my thoughts, and making them a sign to be quiet, I say thus : ' What
now, noisy things, and why such an uproar?
Why so furious and in such a state of strife?
Pray now be still.' Having reëstablished peace
and order with much difficulty, I consider things

with a calm mind, and I see that such wild confusion had its origin in my own discontent. It seems to me that I ought to be quite different from what I am; I can neither please myself nor am I pleased at being what I am at this moment; what wonder, then, that nothing pleases him who cannot please himself?

In order therefore to uproot this painful thought which fills my mind, I make use of the following argument: Tell me, my dearest self, how is it that you, who are made out of nothing, are so foolish as to oppose yourself to the wise law of God, because you think that He ought to have made you a more noble creature than what you are?

Have you any claim to be preferred in creation before all possible men, who have no other existence than to be eternally present to the wisdom of God as possibilities?

Have you not emanated from His sovereign intellect, like some chosen model? Has not God, so to speak, designed and painted you on the vast canvas of the world, and placed you in that position in which at present you find yourself? Whether, then, you are weakly, sickly, miserable, or obscure; rich or poor,

master or servant, whatever you are, you are
such as you are by the Will of God. 'Every
one has his proper gift from God' (1 Cor. vii.).
He has willed you thus; He by whose hands
and by whose voice you are what you are; He
who has made you in such a way that His glory
might be magnified.

Tell me, would it not be ridiculous if the
little figures whom a painter places in his picture, and with a few pencil-strokes sketches in
in the shadow or distance, should begin to cry
out to the artist thus: 'What a clumsy way
you have of doing things! Paint us in brighter
colours, give us a better look, and draw us out
of the dark part of the picture, and place us
more in the light with the other figures! Do
you think it well to make us look so mean and
lost in the distance?' If the painter does not
think it necessary to give these figures a reason
for how he manages his art, or what shades or
lights are necessary in order to give his picture
the different effects which he had proposed to
himself, is God obliged to give a reason to His
creatures?

I. *That God selects that state of life which is most suitable to each person.*

Would it be well if all mankind were to be rich, all kings, or all eminent? Why, the symmetry of the world would be destroyed. What matters it if I am represented in one portion of this great universe in preference to another, provided the part I play serves to show the skill of God, the great master? I see also that God, in His wisdom, knew that my condition of life was the one most suited for me, and the only one which could conduce to my eternal salvation; for in no other state of life would my salvation be so secure, nor in any other state could I so well promote His glory. Why, then, do I not trust myself to His good providence, and adore God and give Him thanks?

Do I really think that He who rules over all things, and weighs and disposes everything with such wisdom, has erred with regard to me alone? I notice that He does not create the tiniest ant without having weighed and provided all that is necessary for such a minute creature; do I then suppose that He,

F

who has created all things for me, does not
know what conduces to my greater good and
to His greater glory? I should be very foolish
if such an extravagant idea entered my head.
Therefore I intend henceforth no longer to
disturb myself with such an idea, but to say,
with a peaceful heart, Whatever I am, I am
from God; and only because I am from God,
I am what I am. And it is good for me to be
thus; nor if I could, would I wish to be otherwise than I am, for fear of opposing so much
wisdom.

CHAPTER XI.

*That he who is content with his state of life ought also
to be content with those things which led to it.*

IF I have spoken faithfully above of resign-
ing myself with tranquillity to that state of life
which Divine Providence metes out to me, it
is also right that I should keep firm the pro-
mise I have made to be resigned also to all
the events which have led me to such a state.
These are of two kinds, external and internal.
External things pertain to our relations, our

country, education, the death of relatives, the favour of friends, the envy of rivals, nobility and obscurity of birth. Internal things pertain to the endowments of mind or of body; as for instance, a lively or idle disposition, a noble or mean spirit, a magnanimous or fearful heart, a good or bad memory, a robust or weak body. Why, then, was I foolishly disturbed by such things, instead of considering the views and dispositions of God? Precisely, because by His providence He intended me to fill a station of mediocrity, He willed that I should be born of poor parents, who had not the means to give me a good education, or to let me apply myself to the higher studies. God ordained that I should gain my livelihood by the sweat of my brow and by the work of my hands, and therefore He made me of low origin, and wished that I should harden my childhood by toiling in a workshop, urged by necessity or by the example of my father. Whence He easily made me familiar with my lot in life, whilst if I had been obliged to encounter the changes of fortune, I should have suffered intolerable pain. If God wished me to be in a humble position, could He have

led me there more gently? And of what use
is it therefore to lament and bewail if prema-
ture death has deprived me of my father, who
could have improved my state of life; or if the
favour of the powerful is denied me; or if I
have lost a lawsuit; or if evil fortune has
everywhere crossed my path? God wishes
me to be a plebeian, poor and abject, and I
kiss my rags, rejoicing to be at the mercy of
God who governs me. You will also, if wise,
be tranquil under those events which may have
led you to that state in which you now find
yourself. 'At durus hic sermo'—'But this is
a hard saying;' and very hard, bitter, and too
biting. According to what you say, then, is
it not lawful to seek to better one's condition,
to deliver oneself from misery, and to raise
oneself from the dust by using honest arts
and just means? Must we wallow in the
mire and crawl in the dust like worms, or be
caged like birds, and not strive to deliver ourselves and fly away? Man tends to greatness
because of his lofty spirit and his noble and
free disposition; you do him injury and destroy his vigour of mind. Indeed! but I have
never forbidden you to seek for your advance-

ment in a lawful manner. I only told you
that you ought not to lose your peace if, after
having made use of the means necessary for
succeeding in your intention, it was not the
will of God that you succeed; for if He does
not wish, though you were to move heaven
and earth, you could not even raise yourself a
hand's breadth from your position. Never wish
to find fault with God respecting the quality
of mind and body which He gives you; nor
complain of the natural ungraciousness of your
disposition, or of the unprepossessing features
of your countenance, or of your variable health,
because God, by such means, determines to
constitute your state. Nor, if you wish to
live happily, must you compare the condition
of others with your own: 'For every one has
his own gift from God, one in one way and
one in another' (1 Cor. vii.), according as He
sees good for each state of life. For if you
wish to compare yourself with others, you
must weigh all the troubles of their state, nor
wish to put them aside and only consider the
happy side; then compare the blessings and
the evils of your state with the blessings and
the evils of those whom you envy, and you

will see clearly that nothing is wanting to you,
and that all has been dealt out to you justly.

———

CHAPTER XII.

*That if we are pleased with our own state of life, we
ought to be pleased with everything belonging to it.*

WHENCE it follows, that if I am content
with my own state of life, I ought not to desire
to add anything with the view of bettering my
condition. It does not seem to me right, because I may wish to have that small comfort
added, or that little bit of nobility, or that tri-
fling honour, or that increase of health, to complain of my Creator, who was so bountiful in
giving me all except that one little thing which
I, ungrateful, seek so eagerly. I am really in
want of nothing, but my own envy torments
me. Thus, if I see that my neighbour lives in
a better style than I do, I immediately begin to
think that I want many things, and I should
bear my poverty contentedly, if he were not
richer than I am. It is, indeed, a shame that
I should be annoyed by the riches of others,

and become ungrateful to my Benefactor, only because He gives more largely to others than to me; He gives me the full measure which suits my state, nor do I require anything more unless my state of life were changed. This is my state, this alone, and no other.

I. *That we ought not to wish to advance our children's state of life, or for them to be in a higher condition.*

That for which I am constantly striving, and which much occupies my thoughts, is to help on my family in the world, and to amass riches for them, so that they may increase in state, nobility, and calling. This is a puerile way of hiding from other people the desire which I have to leave the low station in which God has placed me, and to grow rich and important. What folly and want of faith! Who but God gives me children to take care of? Therefore, He is Lord of me and also of my children. If I am poor, God wishes my sons to be poor, and He wishes them to be born, and to be so numerous, in order that they may be poorer than I am myself.

Let me take care to educate them well, and

provide for them, as is my duty; but I ought to be more anxious still to please His Divine Majesty, and to keep my own soul in peace. During my life I will wish for nothing more than what is fitting for myself and my children; at my death I will trust them to the care of God, who is such a good Father; and why, then, do I go on puzzling my brain, and vexing myself as if God did not exist, or was no longer able to bestow benefits and graces upon men?

Nor must I indulge the vain imagination that I wish to acquire more riches, more dignity, greater knowledge, or of managing great affairs, for the sake of being able to be more liberal, or of acquiring more noble or excellent virtue. This is only folly and pretence. I see plainly that I myself should change with a change of fortune, nor should I wish to do what my imagination now so grandly pictures. The highest talents are as it were surrounded and swallowed up by a whirlpool of many and important affairs, and while those who possess these talents, and are occupied in these concerns, rule others, they neglect themselves. Riches and an expensive way of living harden

the heart instead of softening it, and they render it avaricious and covetous instead of making
it great and liberal. It is difficult to find any
one who is inclined to be merciful to others
unless he is poor himself, for he who wants for
nothing himself is not easily moved by the
wants of others. I learn from all these con-
siderations that I ought to be content with my
poverty, and not wish to change it, because it
is the state in which God wishes me to be; if
I am satisfied with what I am, what can deprive
me of peace?

CHAPTER XIII.

*That we ought to be content with the annoyances incident
to our state of life.*

WHAT can deprive me of peace? Not
poverty, certainly; or being of small impor-
tance amongst men, or possessing little talent,
or small experience in business, or being lame
and of bad carriage, or of not very agreeable
countenance, or timid in manner. It is not
worth while to let such things as these disturb
my peace of mind. But suppose I bear my

misfortunes calmly and bravely, and content with my insignificance, I watch over my actions and cease to disquiet myself, or to give pain to any one, and even help others, and behave kindly to them, still how is it possible that I should bear calmly being ridiculed by idle persons, and abused, calumniated, and persecuted by bad people, with a thousand other injuries and affronts? I can bear to be poor; but I cannot bear to see myself trampled on so rudely.

Friend, I pity you most sincerely, but if you will calm yourself a little, and think of some matters which I offer for your consideration, I am sure that you will join with me in smiling at your own indignation. Do you suppose that any state of life is without its peculiar trials and vexations? If so, you are mistaken. And it would be necessary for us not to be men, if we would not suffer calamity. Whoever is born into this valley of tears must weep; be he king or beggar, he cannot escape the sorrows of this life. He who wishes that the winds should not blow, or the waves be· in motion, does not wish to sail, but to remain in the midst of the ocean without reaching the port. And what are evil tongues, evil speaking, murmurings, calamities, and injurious words—what the hatred of the malevolent, the envy of rivals, the persecutions of enemies, but winds which guide us to our desired haven? The winds may blow, the sea roar, the waves rise, and the whole ocean be in commotion, we will not fear. There sits at the helm a pilot who is Lord over all, and whom the winds and the sea obey. He, calm in His might, and in order to make known His power, let loose that storm, and bid that tempest blow. Therefore, I have no reason to fear. I suffer, but I do not disquiet myself; I suffer, but I am not afraid; for I know well that so many evils would not disturb us, were it not for the opinion that we have of evils, for we often think those things a hindrance which wonderfully assist us in our journey towards eternal happiness. There are many examples of this in sacred Scripture. When the people of Israel groaned in Egypt under every kind of misfortune, and when they gave themselves up for lost on account of the barbarous law ordering all the new-born children to be slain, Moses was placed amongst the rushes by the riverside, and from being well-nigh drowned, he passed to the court, and became the saviour of his people. If Moses had not been put in the river Nile, Israel would have been deprived of a leader. In the height of misfortunes came the salvation of God. And how often has the same thing happened to me, when, by those very circumstances which I considered evils, I have been led to that prosperity to which, perhaps, I should not have attained under more ordinary and peaceful circumstances! Henceforth, if I am wise, I shall commit myself entirely to God, trusting in His love: 'He will not suffer us to be tempted beyond our strength, but will also, with the temptation, make a way of escape' (1 Cor. x.). I will not prescribe the time or the manner of my suffering: I will keep my eye fixed on God alone, and trust to Him who holds me in the palm of His hand, and bowing down reverently before Him, I will kiss that loving hand suppliantly, and while bathing it with my tears I will say: 'The hand of the Lord hath touched me,' and 'in Thy hands is my lot' (Job xix. Ps. xxx.); and from those hands it is my highest happiness to receive favours as well as trials.

CHAPTER XIV.

That we ought not to cease from the labours proper to our state of life.

If I, with great profit to my soul, can feel persuaded that I am placed by Divine wisdom in that state of life which is most suitable for me, and therefore that my condition is the best for me in every way, I must also resolve not to be diverted from any work or labour which belongs to my state of life; for to wish for anything, and not to make use of the means proper for attaining it, is to wish for the impossible, and would be the same thing as wishing to fly without wings. And what kind of blacksmith would he be who, after promising to be fully contented with his occupation, began to feel tired of blowing and stirring the coals which were to make the iron red hot? Or suppose that after heating the iron, he would not draw it out with pincers in order to place it under the anvil, nor fashion it with mallets and hammers? or suppose again that he cast it aside without having first wrought and shaped it with files, and polished it with burnishers? Such a man would only wish to be a blacksmith by name, and not in reality. Every state of life has its own especial work, and it would indeed be folly in any one to give up his own work, and to envy the state of others. If God calls you to the state of matrimony, what use is there in your lamenting that you are not a cenobite, enclosed in a monk's cowl, and singing psalms, and weaving straw-mats? And if by Divine mercy you are a religious, what use is there in complaining of the discipline, the coarse clothing, the retired kind of life, and the singing of psalms; or in envying the life of a merchant, a soldier, or a courtier? And if old age makes you gray, and weakens your circulation and the vigour of your limbs, why do you murmur and envy the freshness, grace, and activity of youth? And if Providence makes you a woman, why do you complain of the weariness of being obliged to occupy yourself with the spindle, the bobbin, or the needle, and wish instead to handle swords and manage horses? God deals out employments most justly, according to age, sex, and condition; why, then, should I feel disturbed at having to do the work necessary for my state of life? I

will do what I am expected to do, and will do
it willingly, and with peace of mind; for God
will not ask of me more than it is fitting for me
to perform. He is just, and requires from me a
just service; He is a father, and requires me
to do my own work, and not that of others.
Because as a father, who sent his son to learn
the work of a goldsmith, would not require of
him other work, such as painting, but would
only require him to learn all that was necessary
for his own especial work with the gold; so in
like manner, God deals with us. He asks each
to do the works of his own state of life, and
not those of others, for 'He will give to every
man according to his works' (Matt. xvi.).

If I am content with my condition, I shall
not refuse the annoyances, troubles, and fa-
tigues which are inseparable from it; nor shall
I be cast down, like one who feels himself op-
pressed by a heavy burden. The blacksmith
does not complain of the weight of the hammer,
or of the smoke from the coal, or of the sound
of the anvil, because these are necessary to the
work, and the iron could not be moulded without them. It would indeed be a new idea if,
on account of fatigue, the neck were to com-

plain of having to support the head, the shoulders the arms; if the bones were to refuse to be clothed with flesh, and the legs declined to carry the body and all its structure above them.

It is necessary, for the sake of the order and economy of mankind, that some should be placed first, others last; that some should have to command, and some to obey; some to rule with wisdom, and others to work: but in every class, in every state, and in every employment, some must aid others, and toil in order to live. But for this, every link which holds society together would be disunited and broken asunder, and human and divine things being in confusion, laws would no longer be holy; nor would the love of one's country, nor the ties of citizenship, nor the incitements to virtue, nor the august authority of religion, be able to restrain such disorder. God, the wise ruler of the universe, wished that everything should fulfil that for which it was created: all creatures obey this law, and shall man alone rebel, and say, 'I will not serve'? Have you ever seen a rose-tree become tired of bearing roses, and ask for a lighter load, such as lilies of the valley? or does the lily wish to bear peonies, the tulip daffodils, and thorn flowers? Each stem peacefully carries that flower with which nature adorns it, just as each tree willingly bears the fruit which nature gives it. The apricot-tree does not wish to change its fruit with the cherry-tree, nor does the peach-tree refuse to bear peaches, nor the bergamot pear-tree wish to exchange with the sultan pear-tree, nor the russet-coloured apple-tree with the rosy-coloured or the apple of paradise; but each bears and takes care of its own fruit, however much it weighs down its branches and draws upon its sap. And shall I not feel satisfied with the tasks annexed to my state, and shall I envy the state of others, as if it were sweeter than my own and less fatiguing? Without labour I should not be what I am, nor do that which I ought to do.

I. *That we ought to rejoice in tribulation.*

As pain is the accompaniment of labour, I will bear it willingly, and will rejoice in the pain, because I suffer with good reason. Weeping, sorrow, and suffering being bequeathed by God to every state of life, I learn that in order to please God I must rejoice, because it is His will that I suffer and pass my days in bitterness. And joy is so deeply rooted in the noblest part of my nature, that while my body is full of suffering, my soul rejoices exceedingly.

This, I know, seems difficult enough to corrupt nature, but he who wishes to rule himself according to reason, and still more according to faith, sees clearly that those grievous and bitter things which he suffers are ordered by the wise providence of God, and he rejoices that they happen, in order that God's divine will may be accomplished. See wherein lies the high mystery, unknown to the uninitiated, of rejoicing because thou rejoicest not; of being full of consolation because thou art deprived of consolation; of being full of joy in the midst of the most desolating bitterness. He who attains to this breathes a pure air, disquieted by no tempest; and while storms are raging around him, he enjoys an unchangeable peace, which gives him happiness to the full.

———

CHAPTER XV.

That lastly we must think of death with a calm mind.

WE have at length reached that climax of human misery which alarms and disturbs the minds of mortals so much, and the thought alone of which changes all happy feelings into unhappy ones, and every joy into bitterness—I mean to say death; which, when considered without reference to Divine Providence, appears the most fearful and dreadful punishment of mankind. We look upon death as very sad, and as injurious to our tranquillity, first, because it deprives us of life and its pleasures; secondly, because it takes us by surprise; thirdly, because we have to suffer from bodily infirmities; fourthly, because our eternal happiness or misery depends upon it. I confess that at first sight the very thought of death filled me with fear and uneasiness; but by degrees my fears ceased, and gave place to reflection. I first began to free my mind from its fears, and when I had gained tranquillity, I was able to view things more calmly. By means of quietly reasoning with myself, I was able to say, If I know that my state is a mortal one, and if in order to conform to God's will, I wish it thus and not otherwise, why should I complain of being obliged to go forward to meet it? Do I think that men ought to be immortal? So then, if I do not conform myself to my condition, I do a plain injury to my God, who wills that I am mortal. Why indeed should I complain of dying more than of living, if it is necessary that whosoever is born must die? And indeed is life so sweet and pleasant, that I should eagerly desire to be spared death? And why do I continually complain of the ills I suffer, if I do not wish to be rid of them? And if I do wish this, why do I dislike death, which mercifully delivers me from so many evils?

It is my own fault that the time of it is uncertain, for I ought not to let a moment pass without preparing to meet it. Thus I ought to be thankful to God that I am ignorant of the time of its arrival, for this is a blessing to me; for if it were given us to know for certain the hour of our death, life would become very unhappy; the continual thought of that fatal moment would poison every pleasure of life. But we live, uncertain of the time of our death, and rejoicing in our happy fortune;

and we rejoice because we do not think of the grim visage of death, and because life appears to us flowery and full of joy.

And coming now to consider infirmities, I say that they are mercifully ordained by God's providence. God loves us as children, and wishes by means of them to soften the passage from life to death. For infirmities cause our vital strength to languish by degrees, and at length we die. Secondly, they cause us to die at the time appointed. Thirdly, they make us more willing to leave a body which is tormented by so many pains, and which is therefore such a disagreeable dwelling-place. Finally, they render death easier to us, for pain stupefies the senses, dulls the imagination, and clouds the mind; it also freezes the blood and diminishes the activity of the limbs; and thus it comes to pass that the spirit departs almost without being aware of it. Why, then, do we find fault with illness, which is so wonderfully planned, in order that we may pass away?

Lastly, there is no reason why I should fear this last moment, but I ought to fear leading an evil life, which alone can render this time terrible to me. Neither do I wish to know when it will come to me, nor do I think it necessary to know it; for in order to prepare myself for it, God does not require that I should act otherwise than I am now acting, if I am now acting well. If death overtakes me while my mind is pure and at peace with God, death will be sweet to me, and I shall welcome it eagerly. When this last moment arrives, I will render thanks quietly to my Lord, my creator and my ruler. When the scene of this life closes, 'I shall lay aside my body like raiment;' and when placed in the tomb of my fathers, 'I shall sleep with them in the dust.'

Meantime 'my conversation shall be in heaven,' until that desired and precious moment arrives, when I shall be with my dearest Saviour, 'who will reform the body of my lowliness, made like to the body of His brightness.' Then 'we shall be with the Lord,' and we shall rejoice exceedingly and for all eternity. God grant that such may be the course, and such the termination of my life!

CONCLUSION.

THEN what is there which I need complain of in my condition? And if there is nothing, why do I not congratulate myself and return thanks to God? Is not this life to be reputed happy, when it leads to eternal happiness? I who am born to such high destinies, shall I wish to be otherwise than I am, when, by means of those very daily things which happen to me, I am being conducted and led to such greatness? Certainly, if while a mortal man, and full of many anxieties, you can say with the poet, 'wish to be what you are, and wish nothing more than this,' you have found the short road to happiness, and also the only true joy of life. Think that you can attain to this in any station, whatever it may be; and if you are content with your own, because it pleases God to place you in it, you are already happy.

Lastly, if you could picture to yourself all possible delights, excepting only those which God reserves for you in heaven, you would not find one which could be compared with the happiness which you feel when satisfied with your state of life. Nor do I exaggerate when I say there is no other true happiness in the world, except that of a soul content with its condition. This is the way to carry heaven about within you, and to be filled with the delights of Paradise in this valley of tears. If you seek elsewhere for happiness, you will seek in vain; and if, from the blindness of your mind, you sometimes think you have attained to it, you will suddenly discover that you only possess a fleeting shadow. Remain therefore firm in your resolution, and wish not for false happiness. You possess true happiness, and you will only find it in a rightly ordered mind.

And as you have seen, we must, in order to have always a right frame of mind, have a high conception of Divine wisdom, for this is the foundation of all human tranquillity. Nor is it necessary for us to search into the reasons of everything in order to keep our mind calm and quiet; it is only necessary to believe firmly that nothing can take place in nature but what is ordered by the divine providence of God.

I know also that when it is given us to contemplate uncreated wisdom 'face to face' in heaven, we shall know the reason of all that

happens in this world; and in the excess of
our joy we shall approve the wonderful designs
of that great mind, and praise them through
all eternity. And this only because we shall
see in heaven with our own eyes those things
which we believe here by faith, and partly also
by our reason. Then we shall be able to join
with the prophet in those holy exclamations of
wonder and of joy: 'Great is the Lord, and to
be praised exceedingly, and holy in all His
works.' O eternal mind, O most sacred
providence and infinite wisdom of God, why
wast thou so long hidden from my view, thou
who dost manifest thyself so wonderfully to
the world? O, how foolish and blind I was!
How great must have been the darkness in
which I was, to obscure such brightness!
What thanks do I owe thee, eternal light of
God, for dispelling the darkness from my eyes,
and for rendering them able to enjoy thy bright
rays. 'Hoc unum de te conqueri possum, quod
non ante mihi voluntatem tuam notam fecisti:
prior enim ad ista venissem, ad quæ nunc
vocatus adsum' (Senec. de Prov. 5)—'This
only can I complain of thee, that thou hast not
made known to me thy will before; for then I

should have gone freely to that to which I am now come when called.' And what more dost Thou seek, and what more dost Thou ask of me, O my God? Is it Thy will to take my children? I offer them to Thee. Dost Thou wish for any part of my body? I give it Thee. I do not anticipate much by so doing, for very soon I shall have to give Thee the whole of it.

Dost Thou wish for my soul? Ah, can I deny it Thee when Thou hast given it? Thou wast able to take it when Thou kindly askedst for it. But why do I say take it? Nothing is taken forcibly but that which is refused. I am forced to nothing, no violence is done to me; I will obey Thee, O Lord, as a son, and not serve Thee as a slave.

Reader, perfection consists in this, not only in bearing the changes of human fortune with patience, but in welcoming them and approving of them. This is true happiness, to wish things to be as they are, and not otherwise; this is the root of that grand 'Thy will be done,' by saying which we not only give God our will, but also our intellect. From this proceeds also the lively, ready, and sincere gratitude, with which we return thanks to our

Almighty Ruler for having so wisely selected for us, amidst all the variety of events, states of life, and fortunes, that state which He judged the most suitable for our eternal safety, and for His greater glory.

What do you say to all this, my readers? Will you at length decide to commit your affairs, without the least hesitation, to the wise providence of God? Will you continue to oppose your judgment, which you see is worth so little, to the Divine will, which has no other object than to render you eternally happy? Where, then, is the esteem in which God's majesty should be held? Where the high conception which you have formed of His infinite wisdom? What! Do you desire that the eternal decrees of God should be decided as you think best? O, do not, I entreat you, wish to do such injury both to your Creator and to yourself. Rather say, with Epictetus, though he was a heathen and deprived of the clear light of grace: 'Tracta me posthac arbitratu tuo, ejusdem tecum sum animi, nihil recuso quod tibi videtur' (apud Aria. 1, 2) — 'Deal with me henceforth according to Thy will, mine is conformed to Thine. I refuse nothing that seemeth to Thee good.' Lead me where Thou willest, clothe me with what pleaseth Thee best. Dost Thou wish me to be a ruler, or willest Thou rather that I should be a private citizen? Am I to lead a quiet life in the midst of my family, or, exiled and banished, shall I pass my days in a foreign land? Am I to be laden with riches and honour, or wilt Thou keep me wrestling with poverty and in protracted misery? Whatever happens to me, I will be on Thy side, O my God, and will take Thy part amongst men, and I will bravely affirm that all happens to me justly: for I shall ever be able to fight better when, lamenting my evil passions, I defend Thy holy decrees.

If, my reader, this Divine sentiment is firmly rooted in your mind, you are already happy and blessed; you have at length found that peace which the world cannot give you; and rejoicing together with you, I will say with the Apostle: 'Rejoice in the Lord always: again I say, rejoice; and the peace of God, which passeth all understanding, keep your hearts and minds in Christ Jesus our Lord. Amen.'

THE END.

A Select Catalogue of Books

PUBLISHED BY

BURNS, OATES, & CO.,

17 & 18, PORTMAN STREET,

AND

63, PATERNOSTER ROW.

BOOKS LATELY PUBLISHED

BY MESSRS.

BURNS, OATES, & CO.,

17 & 18, Portman Street, and 63, Paternoster Row.

———— •◆• ————

Memorials of those who Suffered for the Faith in Ireland in the Sixteenth, Seventeenth, and Eighteenth Centuries. Collected from Authentic and Original Documents by MYLES O'REILLY, B.A., LL.D. 8vo, 7s. 6d.

"A very valuable compendium of the martyrology of Ireland during the three, or rather two, centuries of active Protestant persecution. The language of many of these original records, written often by a friend or relative of the martyr, is inexpressibly touching, often quite heroic in its tone."—*Dublin Review*.

"Very interesting memories."—*Month*.

————

Life of St. Thomas of Canterbury. By Mrs. HOPE, Author of "The Early Martyrs" Cloth extra, 4s. 6d.

A valuable addition to the collection of historical books for Catholic readers. It contains a large collection of interesting facts, gleaned with great industry from the various existing Lives of St. Thomas, and other documents.

"Compiled with great care from the best authors."—*Month.*

"The rich covers of this splendidly-bound volume do not, as is often the case, envelop matter unworthy of its fair exterior. This is a volume which will be found useful as a present, whether in the college or school, for either sex."—*Weekly Register.*

"An agreeable and useful volume."—*Nation.*

"A more complete collection of incidents and anecdotes, combined with events of greater weight, could not be compressed into so compact, yet perfectly roomy, a space."—*Tablet.*

By the same Author.

Life of St. Philip Neri. New Edition.
2s. 6d. ; cheap edition, 2s.

NARRATIVE OF MISSIONS.

The Corean Martyrs. By Canon SHORT-
LAND. Cloth, 2s.

A narrative of Missions and Martyrdoms too little known in this country.

"This is a notice of the martyrs who have fallen in this most interesting mission, and of the history of its rise and progress up to the present day."—*Tablet.*

"No one can read this interesting volume without the most genuine admiration of, and sympathy with, such zeal and constancy."—*Literary Churchman.*

MISSIONARY BIOGRAPHY.

1. *Life of Henry Dorie, Martyr.* Trans-
lated by Lady HERBERT. 1s. 6d. ; cloth, 2s.

"The circulation of such lives as this of Henry Dorie will do much to promote a spirit of zeal, and to move hearts hitherto

BURNS, OATES, & CO., 63, PATERNOSTER ROW, E.C.

stagnant because they have not been stirred to the generous deeds which characterise Catholic virtues."—*Tablet.*

2. *Théophane Vénard, Martyr in Tonquin.*
Edited by the Same.   2s. ; cloth elegant, 3s.

"The life of this martyr is not so much a biography as a series of letters translated by Lady Herbert, in which the life of Théophane Vénard unfolds itself by degrees, and in the most natural and interesting way. His disposition was affectionate, and formed for ardent friendship ; hence, his correspondence is full of warmth and tenderness, and his love of his sister in particular is exemplary and striking. During ten years he laboured under Mgr. Retord, in the western district of Tonquin, and his efforts for the conversion of souls were crowned with singular success. During the episcopate of his Bishop no less than 40,000 souls were added to the flock of Christ, and Vénard was peculiarly instrumental in gathering in this harvest." — *Northern Press.*

"We cannot take leave of this little volume without an acknowledgment to Lady Herbert for the excellent English dress in which she has presented it to the British public ; certainly, no lives are more calculated to inspire vocation to the noble work of the apostolic life than those of Dorie and Vénard."—*Tablet.*

3. *Life of Bishop Brute.*   Edited by the Same.

The Martyrdom of St. Cecilia: a Drama.
By ALBANY J. CHRISTIE, S.J. With a Frontispiece after Molitor. Elegant cloth, 5s.

"Well-known and beautiful drama."—*Tablet.*

"The receipt of the fourth edition of this beautiful play assures us that our own opinion of its merits has been shared by a wide circle of the Catholic public. The binding is exquisite, and the picture of St. Cecilia is a work of art."—*Weekly Register*

The Life of M. Olier, Founder of the Seminary of St. Sulpice; with Notices of his most Eminent Contemporaries. By EDWARD HEALY THOMPSON, M.A. Cloth, 4s.

This Biography has received the special approbation of the Abbé Faillon, Author of " La Vie de M. Olier;" and of the Very Reverend Paul Dubreul, D.D., Superior of the Seminary of St. Sulpice, Baltimore, U.S.

Edited by the Same.

The Life of St. Charles Borromeo. Cloth, 3s. 6d.

Also, lately published, by Mr. THOMPSON.

The Hidden Life of Jesus: a Lesson and Model to Christians. Translated from the French of BOUDON. Cloth, 3s.

" This profound and valuable work has been very carefully and ably translated by Mr. Thompson. We shall be glad to receive more of that gentleman's publications, for good translation, whether from the French or any other language, is not too common amongst us. The publication is got up with the taste always displayed by the firm of Burns, Oates, and Co."—*Register.*

" The more we have of such works as ' The Hidden Life of Jesus,' the better."—*Westminster Gazette.*

" A book of searching power."—*Church Review.*

" We have often regretted that this writer's works are not better known."—*Universe.*

" We earnestly recommend its study and practice to all readers." —*Tablet.*

" We have to thank Mr. Thompson for this translation of a valuable work which has long been popular in France."—*Dublin Review.*

" A good translation."—*Month.*

BURNS, OATES, & CO., 63, PATERNOSTER ROW, E.C.

Devotion to the Nine Choirs of Holy Angels,
and especially to the Angel Guardians. Translated from the Same.   3s.

"We congratulate Mr. Thompson on the way in which he h accomplished his task, and we earnestly hope that an increased devotion to the Holy Angels may be the reward of his labour of love."—*Tablet.*

"A beautiful translation."—*The Month.*

"The translation is extremely well done."—*Weekly Register.*

Library of Religious Biography.   Edited by Edward Healy Thompson.

Vol. 1.   The Life of St. Aloysius Gonzaga, S.J.   5s.

"We gladly hail the first instalment of Mr. Healy Thompson's Library of Religious Biography.   The life before us brings out strongly a characteristic of the Saint which is, perhaps, little appreciated by many who have been attracted to him chiefly by the purity and early holiness which have made him the chosen patron of the young.   This characteristic is his intense energy of will, which reminds us of another Saint, of a very different vocation and destiny, whom he is said to have resembled also in personal appearance—the great St. Charles Borromeo."—*Dublin Review.*

"The book before us contains numberless traces of a thoughtful and tender devotion to the Saint.   It shows a loving penetration into his spirit, and an appreciation of the secret motives of his action, which can only be the result of a deeply affectionate study of his life and character."—*Month.*

Vol. 2.   The Life of Marie Eustelle Harpain; or, the Angel of the Eucharist.   5s.

"The life of Marie Eustelle Harpain possesses a special value and interest apart from its extraordinary natural and supernatural beauty, from the fact that to her example and to the effect of her writings is attributed in great measure the wonderful revival of devotion to the Blessed Sacrament in France, and consequently throughout Western Christendom."—*Dublin Review.*

"A more complete instance of that life of purity and close union with God in the world of which we have just been speaking is to be found in the history of Marie Eustelle Harpain, the sempstress of Saint-Pallais. The writer of the present volume has had the advantage of very copious materials in the French works on which his own work is founded, and Mr. Thompson has discharged his office as editor with his usual diligence and accuracy."—*The Month.*

Vol. 3. THE LIFE OF ST. STANISLAS KOSTKA. 5s.

"We strongly recommend this biography to our readers, earnestly hoping that the writer's object may thereby be attained in an increase of affectionate veneration for one of whom Urban VIII. exclaimed that, although 'a little youth,' he was indeed 'a great saint.'"—*Tablet.*

"There has been no adequate biography of St. Stanislas. In rectifying this want, Mr. Thompson has earned a title to the gratitude of English-speaking Catholics. The engaging Saint of Poland will now be better known among us, and we need not fear that, better known, he will not be better loved."—*Weekly Register.*

The Life of S. Teresa, written by herself: a new Translation from the last Spanish Edition. To which is added for the first time in English THE RELATIONS, or the Manifestations of her Spiritual State which the Saint submitted to her Confessors. Translated by DAVID LEWIS. In a handsome volume, 8vo, cloth, 10s. 6d.

"The work is incomparable; and Mr. Lewis's rare faithfulness and felicity as a translator are known so well, that no word of ours can be necessary to make the volume eagerly looked for."—*Dublin Review.*

"We have in this grand book perhaps the most copious spiritual autobiography of a Saint, and of a highly-favoured Saint, that exists."—*Month.*

The Life of Margaret Mary Alacoque. By the Rev. F. TICKELL, S.J. 8vo, cloth, 7s. 6d.

"It is long since we have had such a pleasure as the reading of Father Tickell's book has afforded us. No incident of her holy life from birth to death seems to be wanting, and the volume appropriately closes with an account of her beatification."—*Weekly Register.*

"It is one of those high-class spiritual biographies which will be best appreciated in religious communities." — *Westminster Gazette.*

"Of Father Tickell's labours we can say with pleasure that he has given us a real biography, in which the Saint is everything, and the biographer keeps in the background."—*Dublin Review.*

"We can only hope that the life may carry on, as it is worthy of doing, the apostolate begun in our country by one who our Lord desires should be 'as a brother to His servant, sharing equally in these spiritual goods, united with her to His own Heart for ever.'"—*Tablet.*

"The work could hardly have been done in a more unpretend-ing, and at the same time more satisfactory, manner than in the volume now before us."—*Month.*

The Day Hours of the Church. Latin and English. Cloth, 1s.

Also, separately,

THE OFFICES OF PRIME AND COMPLINE. 8d.

THE OFFICES OF TIERCE, SEXT, AND NONE. 3d.

"Prime and Compline are the morning and evening prayers which the Church has drawn up for her children; and, for our part, we can wish for nothing better. We know not where an improvement could be suggested, and therefore we see not why anything should have been substituted for them. . . . Why should not their use be restored? Why should they not become the standard devotions of all Catholics, whether alone or in their families? Why may we not hope to have them more solemnly performed—chanted even every day in all religious communities; or, where there is a sufficient number of persons, even in family chapels?"—*Cardinal Wiseman.*

"These beautiful little books, which have received the im-primatur of his Grace the Archbishop, are a zealous priest's answers to the most eminent Cardinal's questions—such answers as would have gladdened his heart could they have been given when first demanded. But the Cardinal lives in his successors

BURNS, OATES, & CO., 17, PORTMAN STREET, W.

and what he so greatly desired should be done is in progress of full performance."—*Tablet.*

" The publication of these Offices is another proof of what we have before alluded to, viz., the increased liturgical taste of the present day."—*Catholic Opinion*

POPULAR DEVOTION.
Now ready.

Devotions for the Ecclesiastical Seasons, consisting of Psalms, Hymns, Prayers, &c., suited for Evening Services, and arranged for Singing. Cloth, 1s. Also in separate Nos. at 2d. each, for distribution, as follows :—

1. Advent and Christmas.	4. Whitsuntide.
2. Septuagesima to Easter.	5. Sundays after Pentecost.
3. Paschal Time.	6. Feasts of our Lady.

7. Saints' Days.

Music for the whole, 1s. 6d.,

" A valuable addition to our stock of popular devotions." —*Dublin Review.*

Church Music and Church Choirs : 1. The Music to be Sung; 2. The proper Singers ; 3. The Place for the Choir. 2s.

" The special value of this pamphlet, and the seasonableness of its circulation, lie in this : that it attempts to solve—and, we believe, does really solve—several important points as to the proper kinds of music to be used in our public Offices, and more especially at High Mass."—*Tablet.*

" We earnestly recommend all who can do so to procure and study this pamphlet."—*Weekly Register.*

" Masterly and exhaustive articles."—*Catholic Opinion.*

BURNS, OATES, & CO, 63, PATERNOSTER ROW, E.C.

f

Liturgical Directions for Organists, Singers,

and Composers. Contains the Instructions of the Holy See on the proper kind of Music for the Church, from the Council of Trent to the present time ; and thus furnishes choirs with a guide for selection. Fcp. 8vo, 6d.

New Meditations for each Day in the Year

on the Life of our Lord Jesus Christ. By a Father of the Society of Jesus. With the imprimatur of his Grace the Archbishop of Westminster. Second Edition. Vols. I. and II., price 4s. 6d. each; or complete in two vols., 9s.

" We can heartily recommend this book for its style and substance ; it bears with it several strong recommendations. . . . It is solid and practical without being dreary or commonplace." *Westminster Gazette.*

" A work of great practical utility, and we give it our earnest recommendation."—*Weekly Register.*

The Day Sanctified : being Meditations and

Spiritual Readings for Daily Use. Selected from the Works of Saints and approved writers of the Catholic Church. Fcp., cloth, 3s. 6d.; red edges, 4s.

" Of the many volumes of meditation on sacred subjects which have appeared in the last few years, none has seemed to us so well adapted to its object as the one before us."—*Tablet.*

" Deserves to be specially mentioned."—*Month.*

" Admirable in every sense."—*Church Times.*

" Many of the Meditations are of great beauty. . . . They form, in fact, excellent little sermons, and we have no doubt will be largely used as such."—*Literary Churchman.*

BURNS, OATES, & CO., 17, PORTMAN STREET, W.

Our Father: Popular Discourses on the Lord's Prayer. By Dr. EMANUEL VEITH, Preacher in Ordinary in the Cathedral of Vienna. (Dr. V. is one of the most eminent preachers on the Continent.) Cloth, 3s. 6d.

" We can heartily recommend these as accurate, devotional, and practical."—*Westminster Gazette.*

" We are happy to receive and look over once more this beautiful work on the Lord's Prayer—most profitable reading."—*Weekly Register.*

" Most excellent manual."—*Church Review.*

Little Book of the Love of God. By Count STOLBERG. With Life of the Author. Cloth, 2s.

" An admirable little treatise, perfectly adapted to our language and modes of thought."—*Bishop of Birmingham.*

NEW BOOK FOR HOLY COMMUNION.

Reflections and Prayers for Holy Communion. Translated from the French. Uniform with " Imitation of the Sacred Heart." With Preface by Archbishop MANNING. Fcp. 8vo, cloth, 4s. 6d.; bound, red edges, 5s.; calf, 8s.; morocco, 9s.

" The Archbishop has marked his approval of the work by writing a preface for it, and describes it as ' a valuable addition to our books of devotion.' We may mention that it contains ' two very beautiful methods of hearing Mass,' to use the words of the Archbishop in the Preface."—*Register.*

" A book rich with the choicest and most profound Catholic devotions."—*Church Review.*

Holy Confidence. By Father ROGACCI, of the Society of Jesus. One vol. 18mo, cloth, 2s.

" As an attack on the great enemy, despair, no work could be more effective ; while it adds another to a stock of books of devotion which is likely to be much prized."—*Weekly Register.*

" This little book, addressed to those ' who strive to draw nearer to God and to unite themselves more closely with Him,' is one of the most useful and comforting that we have read for a long time. We earnestly commend this little book to all troubled souls, feeling sure that they will find in it-abundant cause for joy and consolation."—*Tablet.*

The Invitation Heeded: Reasons for a Return to Catholic Unity. By JAMES KENT STONE, late President of Kenyon College, Gambier, Ohio, and of Hobart College. Cloth, 5s. 6d.

" A very important contribution to our polemical literature, which can hardly fail to be a standard work on the Anglican controversy."—*Dr. Brownson in the New York Tablet.*

₊ Of this able work 3000 have already been sold in America.

The New Testament Narrative, in the Words of the Sacred Writers. With Notes, Chronological Tables, and Maps. A book for those who, as a matter of education or of devotion, wish to be thoroughly well acquainted with the Life of our Lord. What is narrated by each of His Evangelists is woven into a continuous and chronological narrative. Thus the study of the Gospels is complete and yet easy. Cloth, 2s.

" The compilers deserve great praise for the manner in which they have performed their task. We commend this little volume as well and carefully printed, and as furnishing its readers, moreover, with a great amount of useful information in the tables inserted at the end."—*Month.*

"It is at once clear, complete, and beautiful."—*Catholic Opinion.*

Balmez: Protestantism and Catholicism
compared in their Effects upon European Civilisation. Cloth, 7s. 6d.

** A new edition of this far-famed Treatise.

The See of St. Peter. By T. W. ALLIES.
A new and improved edition, with Preface on the present State of the Controversy. 4s. 6d.

Lallemant's Doctrine of the Spiritual Life.
Edited by Dr. FABER. New Edition. Cloth, 4s. 6d.

"This excellent work has a twofold value, being both a biography and a volume of meditations. Father Lallemant's life does not abound with events, but its interest lies chiefly in the fact that his world and his warfare were within. His 'Spiritual Doctrine' contains an elaborate analysis of the wants, dangers, trials, and aspirations of the inner man, and supplies to the thoughtful and devout reader the most valuable instructions for the attainment of heavenly wisdom, grace, and strength."—*Catholic Times.*

"A treatise of the very highest value."—*Month.*

"The treatise is preceded by a short account of the writer's life, and has had the wonderful advantage of being edited by the late Father Faber."—*Weekly Register.*

"One of the very best of Messrs. Burns and Co.'s publications is this new edition of F. Lallemant's 'Spiritual Doctrine.'"—*Westminster Gazette.*

BURNS, OATES, & CO., 63, PATERNOSTER ROW, E.C.

The Rivers of Damascus and Jordan: a Causerie. By a Tertiary of the Order of St. Dominick. 4s.

"Good solid reading."—*Month.*

"Well done, and in a truly charitable spirit."—*Catholic Opinion.*

"It treats the subject in so novel and forcible a light, that we are fascinated in spite of ourselves, and irresistibly led on to follow its arguments and rejoice at its conclusions."—*Tablet.*

Eudoxia: a Tale of the Fifth Century. From the German of IDA, COUNTESS HAHN-HAHN. Cloth elegant, 4s.

"This charming tale may be classed among such instructive as well as entertaining works as 'Fabiola' and 'Callista.' It adds another laurel to the brow of the fair Countess."—*Weekly Register.*

"Instructive and interesting book."—*Northern Press.*

Tales for the Many. By CYRIL AUSTIN. In Five Numbers, at 2d. each; also, cloth, 1s.; gilt edges, 1s. 6d.

"Calculated to do good in our lending-libraries."—*Tablet.*

"We wish the volume all the success it deserves, and shall always welcome with pleasure any effort from the same quarter."—*Weekly Register.*

"One of the most delightful books which Messrs. Burns and Oates have brought out to charm children at this festive season."—*Catholic Opinion.*

In the Snow; or, Tales of Mount St. Bernard. By the Rev Dr. ANDERDON. Cloth neat, 3s. 6d.

"A collection of pretty stories."—*Star.*

"An excellent book for a present."—*Universe.*

BURNS, OATES, & CO., 17, PORTMAN STREET, W.

" A capital book of stories."—*Catholic Opinion.*
" An agreeable book."—*Church Review.*
" An admirable fireside companion."—*Nation.*
" A very interesting volume of tales."—*Freeman.*
" Several successive stories are related by different people assembled together, and thus a greater scope is given for variety, not only of the matter, but also the tone of each story, according to the temper and position of the narrators. Beautifully printed, tastefully bound, and reflects great credit on the publishers."
" A pleasing contribution."—*Month.*
" A charming volume. We congratulate Catholic parents and children on the appearance of a book which may be given by the former with advantage, and read by the latter with pleasure and edification."—*Dublin Review.*

By the same Author.

The Seven Ages of Clarewell : A History of a Spot of Ground. Cloth, 3s.

" We have an attractive work from the pen of an author who knows how to combine a pleasing and lively style with the promotion of the highest principles and the loftiest aims. The volume before us is beautifully bound, in a similar way to ' In the Snow,' by the same author, and is therefore very suitable for a present."—*Westminster Gazette.*
" A pleasing novelty in the style and character of the book, which is well and clearly sustained in the manner it is carried out."—*Northern Press.*
" Each stage furnishes the material for a dramatic scene; are very well hit off, and the whole makes up a graphic picture."—*Month.*
" ' Clarewell ' will give not only an hour of pleasant reading, but will, from the nature of the subject, be eminently suggestive of deep and important truths."—*Tablet.*

WORKS BY LADY GEORGIANA FULLERTON.

Life of Mary Fitzgerald, a Child of the Sacred Heart. Price 1s.; cloth extra, 2s.

BURNS, OATES, & CO., 63, PATERNOSTER ROW, E.C.

WORKS BY LADY GEORGIANA FULLERTON (continued).

Rose Leblanc. A Tale of great interest. Cloth, 3s.

Grantley Manor. (The well-known and favourite Novel). Cloth, 3s.; cheap edition, 2s. 6d.

Life of St. Frances of Rome. Neat cloth, 2s. 6d.; cheap edition, 1s. 8d.

Edited by the Same.

Our Lady's Little Books. Neat cloth, 2s.; separate Numbers, 4d. each.

Life of the Honourable E. Dormer, late of the 60th Rifles. 1s.; cloth extra, 2s.

Helpers of the Holy Souls. 6d.

———

Tales from the Diary of a Sister of Mercy. By C. M. BRAME.

CONTENTS: The Double Marriage—The Cross and the Crown—The Novice—The Fatal Accident—The Priest's Death—The Gambler's Wife—The Apostate —The Besetting Sin.

Beautifully bound in bevelled cloth, 3s. 6d.

" Written in a chaste, simple, and touching style."—*Tablet.*

" This book is a casket; and those who open it will find the gem within."—*Register.*

" Calculated to promote the spread of virtue, and to check that of vice; and cannot fail to have a good effect upon all—young and old—into whose hands it may fall."—*Nation.*

" A neat volume, composed of agreeable and instructive tales.

Each of its tales concludes with a moral, which supplies food for reflection."—*Westminster Gazette.*

"They are well and cleverly told, and the volume is neatly got up."—*Month.*

"Very well told ; all full of religious allusions and expressions."—*Star.*

"Very well written, and life-like—many very pathetic."—*Catholic Opinion.*

"An excellent work ; reminds us forcibly of Father Price's 'Sick Calls.' "—*Universe.*

"A very interesting series of tales."—*Sun.*

By the Same.

Angels' Visits : A Series of Tales. With Frontispiece and Vignette. 3s. 6d.

"The tone of the book is excellent, and it will certainly make itself a great favourite with the young."—*Month.*

"Beautiful collection of Angel Stories. All who may wish to give any dear children a book which speaks in tones suited to the sweet simplicity of their innocent young hearts about holy things cannot do better than send for 'Angels' Visits.' "—*Weekly Register.*

"One of the prettiest books for children we have seen."—*Tablet.*

"A book which excites more than ordinary praise. We have great satisfaction in recommending to parents and all who have the charge of children this charming volume."—*Northern Press*

"A good present for children. An improvement on the 'Diary of a Sister of Mercy.' "—*Universe.*

"Touchingly written, and evidently the emanation of a refined and pious mind."—*Church Times.*

"A charming little book, full of beautiful stories of the family of angels."—*Church Opinion.*

"A nicely-written volume."—*Bookseller.*

"Gracefully-written stories."—*Star.*

Just out, ornamental cloth, 5s.

Legends of Our Lady and the Saints: or, Our Children's Book of Stories in Verse. Written

for the Recitations of the Pupils of the Schools of the Holy Child Jesus, St. Leonards-on-Sea. Cheap Edition, 2s. 6d.

"It is a beautiful religious idea that is realised in the 'Legends of Our Lady and the Saints.' We are bound to add that it has been successfully carried out by the good nuns of St. Leonards. The children of their Schools are unusually favoured in having so much genius and taste exerted for their instruction and delight. The book is very daintily decorated and bound, and forms a charming present for pious children."—*Tablet.*

"The 'Legends' are so beautiful, that they ought to be read by all lovers of poetry."—*Bookseller.*

"Graceful poems."—*Month.*

Edith Sydney: a Tale of the Catholic Movement. By Miss OXENHAM. 5s.

"A novel for the novel-reader, and at the same time it is a guide to the convert and a help to their instructors."—*Universe.*

"Miss Oxenham shows herself to be a fair writer of a controversial tale, as well as a clever delineator of character."—*Tablet.*

"A charming romance. We introduce 'Edith Sydney' to our readers, confident that she will be a safe and welcome visitor in many a domestic circle, and will attain high favour with the Catholic reading public."—*Nation.*

"Miss Oxenham seems to possess considerable powers for the delineation of character and incident."—*Month.*

Not Yet: a Tale of the Present Time. By Miss OXENHAM. 5s.

"The lighter order of Catholic literature receives a very welcome addition in this story, which is original and very striking. The author is mistress of a style which is light and pleasant. The work is one to which we can give our heartiest commendation."—*Cork Examiner.*

"We are indebted to Miss Oxenham for one of the most interesting sensational Catholic tales yet published."—*Catholic Opinion*.

"Wholesome and pleasant reading, evincing a refined and cultivated understanding."—*Union Review*.

"Miss Oxenham's work would rank well even among Mudie's novels, although its one-volume form is likely to be unfavourable in the eyes of ordinary novel-readers ; but, in nine cases out of ten, a novelette is more effective than a regular novel, and any more padding would have merely diluted the vivid and unflagging interest which the authoress of 'Not Yet' has imparted to her elegantly-bound volume. The plot is as original as a plot can be ; it is well laid and carefully and ably worked out."—*Westminster Gazette.*

Nellie Netteville : a Tale of Ireland in the Time of Cromwell. By CECILIA CADDELL, Author of "Wild Times." 5s.; cheap edition, 3s. 6d.

"A very interesting story. The author's style is pleasing, picturesque, and good, and we recommend our readers to obtain the book for themselves."—*Church News.*

"A tale well told and of great interest."—*Catholic Opinion.*

"Pretty pathetic story—well told."—*Star.*

"Pretty book-history of cruelties inflicted by Protestant domination in the sister country—full of stirring and affecting passages."—*Church Review.*

"Tale is well told, and many of the incidents, especially the burning of the chapel with the priest and congregation by the Cromwellian soldiers, are intensely interesting."—*Universe.*

"By a writer well known, whose reputation will certainly not suffer by her new production."—*Month.*

Marie ; or, the Workwoman of Liège. By CECILIA CADDELL. Cloth, 3s. 6d.

"This is another of those valuable works like that of 'Marie Eustelle Harpain.' Time would fail us were we to enumerate either her marvellous acts of charity, or the heroic sufferings she endured for the sake of others, or the wonderful revelations with which her faith and charity were rewarded."—*Tablet.*

"The author of 'Wild Times,' and other favourite works, is to be congratulated on the issue of a volume which is of more service than any book of fiction, however stirring. It is a beautiful work—beautiful in its theme and in its execution."—*Weekly Register.*

"Miss Caddell has given us a very interesting biography of 'Marie Sellier, the Workwoman of Liège,' known in the 17th century as 'Sœur Marie Albert.' Examples such as that so gracefully set forth in this volume are much needed among us."—*Month.*

The Countess of Glosswood: a Tale of the Times of the Stuarts. From the French. 3s. 6d.

"The tale is well written, and the translation seems cleverly done."—*Month.*

"This volume is prettily got up, and we can strongly recommend it to all as an excellent and instructive little book to place in the hands of the young."—*Westminster Gazette.*

"An excellent translation, and a very pretty tale, well told."—*Catholic Opinion.*

"This is a pretty tale of a Puritan conversion in the time of Charles II., prettily got up, and a pleasing addition to our lending-libraries."—*Tablet.*

"This tale belongs to a class of which we have had to thank Messrs. Burns for many beautiful specimens. Such books, while they are delightful reading to us who are happily Catholics, have another important merit—they set forth the claims of Catholicism, and must do a vast deal of good among Protestants who casually meet with and peruse them. The book before us is beautifully got up, and would be an ornament to any table."—*Weekly Register.*

BURNS, OATES, & CO., 17, *PORTMAN STREET, W.*